THE DEAD

DATE DUE

Ireland Into Film

Series editors:
Keith Hopper (text) and Gráinne Humphreys (images)

Ireland into Film is the first project in a number of planned collaborations between Cork University Press and the Film Institute of Ireland. The general aim of this publishing initiative is to increase the critical understanding of 'Irish' Film (i.e. films made in, or about, Ireland). This particular series brings together writers and scholars from the fields of Film and Literary Studies to examine notable adaptations of Irish literary texts.

Other titles available in this series:

This Other Eden (Fidelma Farley)
December Bride (Lance Pettitt)

Forthcoming titles:

The Informer (Patrick F. Sheeran)
The Field (Cheryl Herr)
Nora (Gerardine Meaney)
The Quiet Man (Luke Gibbons)
The Butcher Boy (Colin MacCabe)

Ireland Into Film

THE DEAD

Kevin Barry

CORK **cup** UNIVERSITY PRESS

in association with
THE FILM INSTITUTE OF IRELAND

First published in 2001 by
Cork University Press
Cork
Ireland

British Library Cataloguing in Publication Data
A CIP catalogue record for this book is available from the British Library.

ISBN 1 85918 285 2

Typesetting by Red Barn Publishing, Skeagh, Skibbereen

Printed by ColourBooks Ltd, Baldoyle, Dublin

Ireland into Film receives financial assistance from
the Arts Council / An Chomhairle Ealaíon and the Film Institute of Ireland

For my children

CONTENTS

LIST OF ILLUSTRATIONS

Acknowledgements

I am grateful to the editors of *Ireland into Film*, Keith Hopper and Gráinne Humphreys, for their initiative, advice and guidance. Adrian Frazier, Seán Ryder, Aoife Feeney and Jonathan Williams read the book in typescript and made valuable suggestions. I wish to thank Paul Brennan for allowing me the opportunity to present some early ideas on Huston, Joyce and Rossellini to students of film adaptation at the Sorbonne Nouvelle, Paris III. Also, through a kind invitation from Anne Fogarty, I enjoyed the opportunity to offer a more finished summary of my text at the James Joyce Summer School in Dublin, 2001. I acknowledge the generous support of the Millennium Research Fund of the National University of Ireland, Galway. I offer my thanks to staff of the University's James Hardiman Library and archivists of the Film Institute of Ireland, who have been generous with their patience and knowledge.

The editors would also like to thank Sheila Pratschke, Lar Joye, Michael Davitt, Luke Dodd, Dennis Kennedy, Kevin Rockett, Ellen Hazelkorn, Seán Ryder, Dan O'Hara, St Cross College (Oxford), the School of Irish Studies Foundation and the Arts Council of Ireland. Special thanks to Tony Huston for allowing access to his screenplay.

The publishers wish to thank Kramsie Productions for permission to reproduce Plates 9–13 and Carlton International for all other images reproduced herein.

1

READERS AND VIEWERS
....

Film gives back to the dead a semblance of life, a fragile semblance, but one immediately strengthened by the wishful thinking of the viewer.
Christian Metz, 1985[1]

James Joyce's short story 'The Dead' has provoked conflicting readings. The story has been read as a vicarious autobiography, as a ghost story in which the dead take revenge upon the living, as an instance of epiphany, as a work of Flaubertian realism, as a work of Mallarméan symbolism, as a competition between imperial patriarchy and wild Irish otherness, and as an exemplary tale of mate rape.[2] Some interpret the words about setting out on a journey westward to be a simple declaration that Gabriel Conroy will alter his holiday plans and go to Galway instead of France; others read the same words as a commitment to a new cultural politics; others again read this gesture as a wish for death. Hugh Kenner made available a powerful hypothesis that the story is a model of indeterminacy, a texture of loose ends, which begins and ends with phrases that we cannot with any certainty attribute to the narrator of the story, or to its characters, or to its author.[3]

'The Dead' was Joyce's last short story. He completed it in 1907 and then moved on to larger novelistic forms. John Huston's *The Dead* was Huston's last film. It was screened at the Venice and Dublin film festivals in the months immediately after Huston's death on 28 August 1987. John Huston's *The Dead* has received, on the whole, a more settled interpretation than Joyce's story. This is because the film's style stabilizes many of the verbal complexities and narrative loose ends of Joyce's story. However, certain differences in interpretation of Huston's film have been striking. These differences tend to be highly specific. For example, viewers have been divided over the film's closing images: for some, the scenes of snow, river, gravestones and a round tower look like family snaps 'shown to neighbours on return from a winter holiday';[4] for others, they are part of an Irish nationalist iconography, and a revelation of Joyce's political unconscious. Viewers differ also about the status of Aunt Julia (Cathleen Delany) singing 'Arrayed for the Bridal': some argue that Huston cherishes her performance; others make comparisons with a strangled cat. The climactic appearance of Gretta (Anjelica Huston) alone on the stairs has been judged to entail a loss of mystery, because she is so visible to Gabriel (Donal McCann), so close to the camera, and so clearly lit. The same scene has been judged to be a shrewd mediation of the original story for viewers unfamiliar with Joyce's text. Some allege that the addition of a recitation of 'Donal Óg' by a Mr Grace (Seán McClory) contradicts Joyce's cultural politics; others judge it to be an apt and necessary anticipation of the singing of 'The Lass of Aughrim'.

Huston's film is one of the most tactful readings of Joyce's 'The Dead'. It is also a strong *mis*reading. First, the film is deeply informed by a humanist literary critique of Joyce's story. Second, the film dislocates Joyce's story into a new medium: cinema. As such, it translates the story out of Joyce's and into Huston's *oeuvre*, to which it has served as epitaph. The film in 1987 reworked Joyce's story in a new historical context: not least that of an Irish nation-state that had not existed when Joyce composed 'The Dead' eighty years previously. John Huston's *The Dead* is one of several defining moments in the filmic representation of Irish life in international cinema. Joyce and Huston, in their presentation of this story, shared a common and specific intention: to call into question accepted stereotypes of Ireland abroad. Joyce was humiliated when, in Trieste in 1906, he 'heard the little Galatti girl sneering at [his] impoverished country'. He added 'The Dead' to *Dubliners* after he had judged that his collection of stories might be 'unnecessarily harsh'.[5] John Huston was determined that the film *The Dead* would serve to counteract bleak and exotic images of Ireland, whether on the New York stage or in John Ford's *The Quiet Man* (1952).[6]

Funding for *The Dead* derived from the USA, from Germany and from England. The cost of production was extraordinarily low: $3,500,000. The film, after its launch, tended to be screened on the art house circuit and in smaller cinemas, except in Ireland where it played to relatively larger audiences. Reviewers welcomed the film's serenity. A photograph of Huston, dying of emphysema, directing from a wheelchair, lent the film the authority of a man's dying words. Comparison was made with Luchino Visconti, who, during the last years of his life, had directed *Conversation Piece* (1974) from a wheelchair.[7] Viewers sought to explain the structure of *The Dead* by comparing the film to a cantata or to a 'chamber music composition of the rarest delicacy'.[8] At least one critic discovered similarities with *Fanny and Alexander* (1982) by Ingmar Bergman, a director whom Huston held in the greatest respect.[9] Irish audiences in the late 1980s were pleased to discover a serene image of Irish life. Such an image stood out as a contrast to a media profile of endemic Irish violence and renewed Irish poverty, after almost twenty years of conflict in Northern Ireland, with emigration again on an upward curve and with a per capita external debt among the highest in Europe.

In the overlapping contexts of Irish cinema and of international cinema about Ireland, Huston's film has an appropriately awkward status. He had become an Irish citizen, renouncing his US citizenship, in 1964. The film is, therefore, directed by an Irishman and uses an extraordinary number of Irish crew. However, recent studies of Irish cinema firmly place *The Dead* in the context of international cinema about Ireland, and this is judged defensible because funding derived from international production companies that had the US for their axis. In 1987 US productions held 87% of the Irish distribution market and during the 1980s this remained the average figure and the highest percentage in Europe. Also in 1987, the Irish government closed down Bord Scannán na hÉireann, the first Irish Film Board, which had been inaugurated in 1981 and had managed to repay only 8% of monies invested by the state. Indigenous Irish film production remained at a low level throughout the 1980s, averaging four films annually, one-third of the annual production of Denmark, one-thirtieth of that of either France or Italy.[10]

The dominance of international and, in particular, of US production finance has decided the representation of Ireland on screen. Such representation has taken two main generic forms: the wilderness romance of *Man of Aran* (1934), *The Quiet Man* (1952), *Ryan's Daughter* (1970) or *The Field* (1990); and the violent political melodrama of *The Informer* (1935), *Odd Man Out* (1947), *The Long Good Friday* (1979) or *Michael Collins* (1996).[11] The exotic landscapes of the wilderness romance are those of the primitive West, of the Aran Islands and of Connemara, settings in which Molly Ivors, with her cultural nativism, might find congenial work as a Locations Manager. The cityscapes of the violent political melodrama are the shadowed laneways, empty warehouses and public edifices, where heroes lurk, betray and pose as beautiful incendiaries. *The Dead* sets aside both these generic forms. Huston's film, with its surprising restraint, its urban politeness, its unspectacular action, represents the Irish not as violent men and women but as experts in small-scale conflict resolution. And it represents Ireland as a place of social custom in which wilderness romances, such as that of Michael Furey, are remembered only on those occasions when an old ballad is sung at the end of a long night.

This book is written for readers who are familiar with both the story and the film. It is at moments of apparent similarity that story and film can be analysed as distinctly different in kind, perhaps most at odds with one another at those moments when we take their identity for granted. In order to avoid taking for granted the identity laconically proposed in their common title, The Dead, my analysis will recognize the distinctive structures and contexts of Joyce's story and Huston's film. I also introduce other film variations, by Roberto Rossellini and by Woody Allen, that freely develop the narrative dilemma that 'The Dead' has presented to its innumerable readers.

2

THE STRUCTURE OF JOHN HUSTON'S *THE DEAD*

John Huston decided to make a film of 'The Dead' more than thirty years before he secured production funding. In Ireland in 1956, to film one of America's founding fictions, *Moby Dick*, Huston first resolved upon a project that would be his last, the filming in America of one of Ireland's founding fictions, 'The Dead'.[12] On 3 September 1987 John Huston's *The Dead* had its world première at the Venice Film Festival, just a short train ride up the Adriatic coast from Trieste, where the story had been written eighty years previously. The Dublin Film Festival, in late October, was the occasion of the Irish première. Huston had died at Newport, Rhode Island, on 28 August. Reviewers did not fail to refer to *The Dead* as his epitaph.[13]

Huston's career can be read as one instance of the romantic principle that great artists live a life of allegory and their works are the comments on it.[14] Huston's movies are comments on a life of spectacular adventure: a boxer in California; a story writer, actor, journalist and theatre director in New York; a horseman in the Mexican cavalry; a student of painting and a street artist in Paris; a writer and movie director in Hollywood; a recipient of the Legion of Merit in the United States Armed Services in 1944; a renegade to the

Plate 1.

American film industry after 1950; a resident of Galway from 1955, of Mexico from 1972; an Irish citizen from 1964; a man five times divorced.[15] Many of Huston's films, though adapted from the fiction of other writers, work the territories of his autobiography: the paintings of Toulouse-Lautrec in *Moulin Rouge* (1953); military cowardice and heroics in *The Red Badge of Courage* (1951); the horses of *The Misfits* (1961); the boxers of *Fat City* (1972); the Mexico of *Under the Volcano* (1984); family self-destruction in *Prizzi's Honor* (1985).[16]

The Dead also revisits Huston's life and times. In his autobiography, *An Open Book* (1980), he had recalled the customs of civility at his home, St Cleran's, in County Galway. Memorable Christmas and Boxing Day parties with 'plum pudding made in October and carefully mellowed in brandy', musical performances and exchanges of gifts with family and friends:

It was a world apart. The style of life was charming. People dressed for dinner – women in long gowns, men in black ties or even formal attire . . . It was as beautiful and as fantastic as a masquerade. We ate dinner by the light of fifty candles, and in the winter the hearth was always going. This was a life style that had existed for hundreds of years, but by the time I moved to Ireland it was already a dying tradition.[17]

The Dead remembers that lost milieu with nostalgia. Furthermore, the film registers Huston's life at the time of filming Joyce's story. The opening credits, with their shadow play of faded and bright typography, their counterpoint of embodied and ghostly light, end with the enigmatic, off-centre and italicized phrase: *for Maricela*. This gesture, which may be echoed in the monitory, off-centre presence of Lily (Rachael Dowling) at intense moments in the film's narrative structure, binds *The Dead* to the last years of Huston's life. For by this gesture Huston dedicates *The Dead* to his last and, in his own words, his most beloved companion, an illegal alien in the United States, Maricela Hernandez, a Mexican who had worked as a maid to Huston's fifth wife, Cici.[18]

Although *The Dead* is a film of a relatively polite and delimited world, it should not therefore be viewed as a reversal of Huston's established directorial methods, a restrained swansong after a swashbuckling life and *oeuvre*. *The Dead* continues the filmic practices that Huston had used in the tougher surroundings of *The Maltese Falcon* (1941), in his Cuban film *We Were Strangers* (1949), in the tenements of *The Asphalt Jungle* (1950), on board *The African Queen* (1952), in the interiors of truck, house or saloon bar in *The Misfits*, in the boxing ring and in the diner of *Fat City*. Manny Farber best described the distinctive film style of static portraiture that sets Huston apart from a classic Hollywood practice of unbroken scenic action. His summary account appeared more than fifteen years before

The Dead was made, but it has uncanny accuracy to its directorial method:

> Huston's art is stage presentation, based on oral expression and static composition: the scenery is curiously deadened and the individual has an exaggerated vitality . . . The Huston trademark consists of two unorthodox practices – the statically designed image (objects and figures locked into various pyramid designs) and the mobile handling of close three-figured shots. The Eisenstein of the Bogart thriller, he rigidly delimits the subject matter that goes into a frame, by chiaroscuro or by grouping his figures within the square of the screen so that there is hardly room for an actor to move an arm: given a small group in close quarters, around a bar, bonfire, table, he will hang on to the event for dear life.[19]

All these features characterize *The Dead*: portraiture in the shots of Mrs Malins (Marie Keane) and of Gretta on the staircase (Plates 1

Plate 2.

and 3), oral expression and pyramid composition in the scene where Gretta, changing her boots, converses with Gabriel's aunts (Plate 4); exaggerated individual vitality and deadened scenery in the shot of Freddy Malins (Donal Donnelly) (Plate 5); stage presentation of characters to one side and foregrounded in an exchange between Gretta and Gabriel about Molly Ivors (Maria McDermottroe) (Plate 6); mobile handling of close three-figure shots when Mr Browne (Dan O'Herlihy) presents his gift on arrival (Plate 7); chiaroscuro in the shot of Gretta in her night-dress in the hotel bedroom (Plate 15); rigid delimitation of crowded space in the guests' efforts to have Aunt Kate (Helena Carroll) sit down and stop fussing (Plate 8); patient observation of an uncomfortably compacted group in the shots of the dinner table before, after and during Gabriel's speech (Plate 18). The film's lengthening of the party scenes, relative to Joyce's story, shows Huston hanging on to these crowded events 'for dear life'.

In any description of the static staging of individuals and groups in Huston's movies, we must also record his recurrent use of the camera to define the attitude of listening. The posture of a character listening, in rapt, or absent-minded, or shrewdly ironic attention, is a Huston signature. In *The Dead*, the camera moves slowly across the several young 'ladies' who are listening to Mr Grace's recitation. The guests around the table attend eagerly to Gabriel's speech (Plate 2). The camera lingers on Gretta as she listens to 'The Lass of Aughrim' (Plate 3). And, of course, Gabriel fills the screen when he listens to his own monologue at the film's ending. The act of listening links *The Dead* to many other Huston movies: from his directorial debut when the attitude of listening in *The Maltese Falcon* characterizes Sam Spade and establishes his position of shrewd authority over his too-talkative antagonists. So too, in *The Dead*, Gretta comes to establish her evolving status as protagonist by repeated attitudes of listening. Listening is the attitude of her most distracted moments (patient, intense, or absent-minded) at the party, on the stairs and in the carriage.

A cinema of such patient stasis is faced with extraordinary difficulties in deriving pleasure for the film's spectators from the very few scenic and character options that are available in *The Dead*. The interior settings are deliberately undifferentiated in their decor: staircase, landing, reception rooms and hotel bedroom. The exteriors are minimal: the house-front is seen from a single angle three times; the quayside and monochrome streetscape serve as a transition to the interior of the hotel stairs and bedroom. The greater length of the film is spent at the party, where only the staircase, bathrooms and reception rooms are usable as *mise-en-scène*. The action also is limited in range: verbal exchanges, repeated dance sequences, the ceremony of serving food, the performance of party pieces (Mary Jane's, Mr Grace's, Aunt Julia's, Gabriel's, Bartell D'Arcy's) and the performance of traumatic memory (Gretta's, in the hotel bedroom). The guests, too, are derived from a deliberately restricted palette, with youth and age, men and women, being the main categories of difference and sameness.

Given the film's evenness of tone, sameness is the quality that most threatens the screen. Indeed, the film's Director of Photography, Fred Murphy, reported that 'The hard part was trying to figure out what to do with all the black tuxedos! There's a crowd of people, half of whom are wearing jet-black tuxedos.' Murphy's solution to lighting the set deserves extensive quotation:

> For the lights, I used a combination of large 6,000 watt silver-tipped bulbs, hung off to the sides of the set. They're called coop lights. Each wall basically had a couple of coop lights in it . . . That creates a wall of light coming across the set *but*, due to the nature of the costumes and the set itself, it doesn't appear as if that is what's being done [to light the scenes]. The costumes are so dark, and the walls are so complicated and dark, it appears as if the light is not from one large source, but several. It doesn't look flat-lit, but like

a much more complicated source of light . . . There are warm tones, browns, yellows, ochres, with occasional greens and black. In a certain way, the film is almost monochromatic. By eliminating most of the colder tones, except at the beginning and end when they [the departing guests] go outside, it has a very dark kind of rich, black-and-white look to it . . . I filled the faces in a bit with bounce light. There are also assorted spotlights creating highlights on walls or effects on tables. But, basically, the entire movie is lit by a large, soft source, about 90 degrees or more opposed to the camera. There are so many candles, oil-lamps, chandeliers, and sconces in every room. That means that the light is rarely coming from a particular source; you see so many light sources in every shot. So I used that to continuously back- or side-light things. In one sense, it's a very simple lighting.[20]

Within the deliberate tonal limits established by Production Designer Stephen Grimes, Costume Designer Dorothy Jeakins and Set Decorator Josie MacAvin, we can notice the division of the film by simple systems of contrast, such as that, for example, of windows. The film opens with the house-front, seen from the cold snow-covered street, vividly realized by the yellow light that defines the geometry of its three first-floor windows and its Georgian fanlight. This same shot is repeated three times: to mark the arrival of guests at the party, to measure the passing of time and to mark the guests' departure. It signals always the contrast between warm life within the house and cold dark silence without. That contrast is the constitutive theme in the recitation of Mr Grace, in the words of the song 'The Lass of Aughrim' and in Gretta's story about Michael Furey. Windows serve as a filament, separating inside from outside, and at the same time acting as a signal to the world without of the pleasure that lies within.

Plate 3.

Doors open and close, but windows that pour out light may always be inviting and available to the world.

Conversely, at the film's end, the darkened hotel room allows Gabriel to look out on the world through a window that emits no radiance into the world. In Joyce's story, windows serve as instances of a simple contrast: Gabriel looks out from the window of the drawing-room, and Michael Furey throws gravel at Gretta's window in Galway. Huston, however, regulates this system more fully and introduces a third element: in the film, the stained-glass window that frames Gretta as she stands listening on the stairs radiates light within as no other window does (Plate 3). By means of such repetition and variation, the film elaborates contrastive visual systems that derive from, and add to, basic narrative elements within the story itself.

Mobility of camera and movement within the frame are exploited by Huston in order to counterpoint static methods of portraiture and stage presentation. The camera acts as if it were a privileged guest free to move around the rooms, the staircases and upstairs to Aunt Julia's room. The camera does not give precedence to one point of view. In spite of the self-imposed limitations of scene and action,

> It is a motion picture full of motion. When the camera is still and the editing leisurely, the frame is full of moving figures, when the figures are still, the camera moves and the pace of the editing is likely to increase. The four-hundred-odd shots of the narrative average about eleven seconds, but very few individual shots are of average length. Huston's sense of rhythm is evident in the lively, varied pacing of the narrative and in the cinematography and editing. The greater part of running time is occupied by long takes, often sustained through multiple camera movements.[21]

Repetition and variation constitute the key pattern of the film. This pattern is required by the film's adoption of a classic Hollywood narrative style for a story that lacks the momentum of a plot to drive the action forward.

Classic Hollywood style had been in part Huston's invention. *The Maltese Falcon* stands as an exemplary instance of classic film narration. The logic of cause and effect decides *mise-en-scène*, chronology, continuity editing, cutting of shot/reverse-shot, framing, distinctive character functions and clarity of plot resolution. Its sequences of action result from causes that are largely psychological and explicable within the motivations provided by the value of the fabulous bird, and by the detective's commitment to his job. That narrative line coincides with another: the sexual attraction of Sam Spade to Brigid O'Shaughnessy. The demands of each narrative line are resolved (with different emotional tensions) in the final scenes of the movie. The static methods preferred by Huston (such as portraiture, stage presentation, delimitation of crowded space and chiaroscuro) are dynamically activated by a narrative suspense that captivates the

Plate 4.

movie's spectators.[22] *The Dead*, by contrast, lacks narrative suspense. Repetition and variation, therefore, become the structural pattern Huston employs to establish micro-sequences of suspense, continuity and coherence. It is for this reason, no doubt, that reviewers expressed their admiration for the film by comparing it to a piece of chamber music or a cantata.

The sequence of repetition and variation is tripartite. On a large scale we can divide the film into three main events (arrival, party, hotel room); three defeats (for Gabriel, through the words of Lily, Molly Ivors and Gretta); three performances (Mary Jane's, Mr Grace's, and Aunt Julia's); three moments of reverie for Gretta (at Mr Grace's recitation, at Aunt Kate's passionate words about the English tenor, Parkinson, and at Bartell D'Arcy's singing of 'The Lass of Aughrim'). This large-scale structure functions to ensure narrative coherence, but it does not itself animate the narrative. That is the function of the micro-sequences, each of which is itself a tiny narrative. The three elements that constitute each micro-sequence are: apprehension, irresolution and ceremonial movement. Variations on these elements include: contradiction (in place of apprehension), deflection (in place of irresolution), arrest or stasis (instead of ceremonial movement). Each micro-sequence then contains suspense and progression: suspense, because each apprehension requires resolution; progression, because in the overall scheme of the film each succeeding apprehension or contradiction becomes more difficult to resolve; and ceremonial movement more difficult to re-establish.

The pattern defines itself from the beginning with the cut from the establishing shot of the outside of the house to the unexplained anxious behaviour on the stairs of Aunt Kate and Aunt Julia at the arrival of guests. This apprehension is briefly resolved: Aunt Kate names its cause – that Gabriel is late – and hopes that he will arrive before Freddy Malins. The ceremonial movement then follows with the warm politeness of greeting those who have arrived, Miss Furlong (Katherine O'Toole), Miss Higgins (Bairbre Dowling) and Miss O'Callaghan (Maria Hayden). Immediately, another small anxiety occurs with a question about the whereabouts of Mary Jane (Ingrid Craigie) and mention of a piano lesson that has been missed. This anxiety is partly quelled by reassurance from Aunt Kate, and the cut to Mary Jane elegantly carrying a plate of food from the kitchen. Apprehension occurs again with the query from Lily about how she can manage to watch the potatoes and answer the hall door. This query is left hanging by the ceremony of greeting Mr Kerrigan (Cormac O'Herlihy) and Mr Bergin (Colm Meaney), and is resolved in Mary Jane's advice that Lily do her best. All this in its turn is followed by further greetings.

The opening of the hall door prompts a repetition of the original anxiety, and that is now assuaged with the reassurances of Mr Browne's voice. This micro-sequence ends with the ceremonious giving of Epiphany gifts. A new playful anxiety is Mr Browne's pretence that he feels insulted, an anxiety which is salved with several reassurances. A ring on the doorbell again raises nerves and the arrival of Gretta and Gabriel is marked by his excuse because they are late. This is resolved in the warm greeting the aunts offer Gretta. The film now moves for the first time from apprehension to contradiction in the exchange between Gabriel and Lily, who, we may notice, has been the one connecting link between these micro-sequences. The contradiction is not resolved, but is deflected by the inadequate ceremony of his giving her money and declaring, in reply to her attempted refusal, that it is Christmas. This moment of failure is followed by a cut to the ceremonial movement of the dancing of undifferentiated guests, after which the sequential pattern can begin once more. The camera finds Gabriel doubtfully reading over the words of his speech and, after his irresolute rehearsal of a couple of sentences, the sequence resolves in the cut to the ceremony of the two aunts chatting with Gretta as she adjusts her stockings and changes into her party shoes. Renewed apprehensions about Lily, about Gabriel's speech and other minor differences, such as the famous galoshes, unwind in the taking of punch. The first part of the film, the arrival, concludes with Freddy Malins. Initial apprehension about his being drunk is left hanging in the ceremonial movement of Gretta dancing with Bartell D'Arcy (Frank Patterson) to the tune of 'The Mountains of Mourne'. Freddy's dishevelment and his anxiety about relieving himself 'in the presence of another' dissolves in chatter about Moore's *Irish Melodies* and medicinal drink, and further dancing.

In this way a pattern of variation and repetition is established and this can be traced though all the succeeding scenes. The first section of the film, the arrival, had begun in anxiety and resolved itself in the protocols of the party, in the ceremonial movement of waltzes and quadrilles. The second section, the party itself, begins in Gabriel's uneasy distraction from Mrs Malins as he looks up at Gretta waltzing.

The party resolves itself with the ceremonies of dinner and departure. The final section, the hotel bedroom, begins with Gabriel's unease about what Gretta might be thinking and resolves itself with his voice-over, and the collage of images and Alex North's musical score that confirm Gabriel's words. Within each section the moment of apprehension becomes more and more acute. This can be

Plate 5.

demonstrated in the three performances that define the progress of the party. The first performance, by Mary Jane playing the piano, raises the very simple apprehension that its hectic delivery is going to go on for ever. The reaction shots show faces unmoved by her playing. Anxiety is resolved in the ready applause that immediately follows when her performance at the piano stops. The second performance, by Mr Grace, has the same filmic structure of delivery, reaction shots and resolution. However, the recitation, by its unexpected intensity (tragic instead of comic, as he warns his audience), introduces a danger of irresolute stasis that must be deflected. On this occasion the party audience, by contrast with their response to Mary Jane's piano solo, do not know how to release themselves from their response to the dramatic monologue. Silence, stillness, irresolute words hang in the air. Gabriel deflects the issue by applause. Gretta shakes herself out of this, her first distracted trance. Lily (who has been standing unmoved in deep focus) announces that the goose will be ready in half an hour. 'Now back to the dancing,'

Plate 6.

announces Aunt Kate, as she leads Gabriel into the arms of Miss Ivors.

Readers of the story and viewers of the film are familiar with these moments of difficulty that occur during the evening: Gabriel's row with Molly Ivors about the West of Ireland, his abruptness with Gretta, the outburst against the Pope banning women from church choirs, the untimely request by Mr Browne for apple sauce, the canonical difficulties about Mount Melleray, the unanswered question of whether or not a black man can have an excellent tenor voice. The film integrates these moments into the structure of apprehension or contradiction, irresolution or deflection, ceremonial movement or stasis. This structure transforms some moments that are of less ambiguous status in Joyce's story, such as Aunt Julia's singing of 'Arrayed for the Bridal'. Those in charge of the film considered several options before deciding to have Cathleen Delany, the actress who plays Aunt Julia, herself sing this demanding piece by George Linley after Vincenzo Bellini.[23] Viewers of the film have been divided about her performance. Clive Hart is of the opinion that, 'The producers chose to have Julia sing ill, turning a fine artistic moment into a piece of banal pathos. It is, I think, my single most serious criticism of the production.'[24] Denis Donoghue takes a diametrically opposite view:

> The finest performance, and the one directed with most convincing tact, was Cathleen Delany's as Aunt Julia. The scene in which she is persuaded to sing 'Arrayed for the Bridal' . . . is a choice instance of finesse. It could have been dreadful; it would have been easy to parody the old woman and show her singing as an absurdity. But Huston presented her as the ruin of a once fine voice and still enough of a musician to know what a better performance of the aria would be.[25]

The function of Cathleen Delany's singing is precisely its uncertain authority. For this uncertainty, shared by the cinema and the party audience, and the motive for Freddy's excessive praise of her performance, is simply another instance of the pattern of apprehension and irresolution that constitutes the structure of the film. If Aunt Julia had sung like Joan Sutherland or if she had sung atrociously, neither could have served the film's structural demand for moments of apprehension and irresolution. Uncertainty in the film lends suspense to what is merely a descriptive moment in Joyce's story, in which readers are assured that the singer, 'strong and clear in tone . . . did not miss even the smallest of the grace notes'.

The structural rhythms of the film remain quite distinct from those of Joyce's text.[26] For example, Joyce had not marked with any particular emphasis the praise that Aunt Kate, at the dinner table, gives to the tenor Parkinson. The film, by contrast, transforms this moment by aligning it within the sequence of performances by Mr Grace and Aunt Julia through the camera's distinctive management of irresolution, response and deflection. Aunt Kate's rapt words about the pure, sweet, mellow, English tenor voice of Parkinson bring the conversation about great dead singers to a conclusion, structurally and affectively identical to that of Mr Grace's recitation. Both conclusions hang in irresolute silence and stillness. The focus of attention in both is a close-up of a woman's ecstatic face, and the distracted absorption of Gretta in the words that have been spoken. The threat of stasis in both scenes is deflected by Lily. Now, as Aunt Kate's words hang in the air, Lily announces that pudding is ready to be served.

Such a change of structural rhythm from story to film has, of course, ideological consequences. The film's strongly patterned parallelism between a Gaelic tale retold by Mr Grace and an English tenor voice recalled by Aunt Kate subverts any contrast that idealizes West over East, Gaelic Ireland over England. The recurrence of Lily at key moments also has ideological consequences that are structurally marked as contrasts of social class. Joyce's story has little use for Lily after the guests arrive. Huston's film, however, places Lily at the departure and at the arrival of the guests, and her presence and her practical advice in the drawing-room and dining-room counterpoint the sensibility of the ladies and the gentlemen. When Gabriel is watching from the hallway as Gretta listens to 'The Lass of Aughrim' from the stairs, Lily surveys both with her neutral eye and then walks out of the frame, leaving the gentleman to his sensibility and his fate.

The structure of repetition and variation defined by the film works also to ensure that it produces a sensation of serenity. That serenity is prepared for throughout the film by its systematic use of musical instrumentation. The piano corresponds to ceremony without sensibility, as in Mary Jane's performance and also the quadrilles at the moment of Gabriel's row with Miss Ivors. Passionate sensibility is marked in the film by two different kinds of music: bowed stringed instruments and the singing voice. Viewers of the film may notice the sudden surge of strings when Aunt Kate finishes her ecstatic words about Parkinson, or the continuation of Bartell D'Arcy's singing voice into a warm brief surge of strings as Gretta gathers herself together and descends the stairs. These strings continue into the carriage shared by Gretta and Gabriel, are silenced by the inept story of Johnny the horse, and return to reinforce Gabriel's final monologue. The film's serene resolution of the differentiated timbres of the piano, on the one hand, and bowed strings or the singing voice, on the other, is the music of the harp. The harp, a stringed instrument that resonates by a plucking of the strings, is the marker of a serenity in which the film begins and ends. The opening and closing credits appear and disappear on screen as a harp plays the melody of 'The Lass of Aughrim'. As the credits themselves come to an end, the film finally bids viewers a warm and ceremonious farewell with a richly orchestrated waltz tune played on a variety of stringed and wind instruments.

3

STILL FAITHFUL AFTER EIGHTY YEARS

The day John Huston was born in Missouri, James Joyce was for the first time viewing the ruins of the Roman forum. Joyce was twenty-four years old. It was 5 August 1906, a Sunday, his only day off work at the bank. He was distressed by the accents of North American tourists (or, as he describes it, 'a party of Murrican gorls'), who may quite possibly have travelled from Missouri. Within days, wishing to return to the less pretentious world of Trieste, Joyce gave his dislike of Rome and its tourism sharper focus: 'Rome reminds me of a man who lives by exhibiting to travellers his grandmother's corpse.' Within weeks he felt the eternal city was getting the better of him: 'Nothing surprises, moves, excites or disgusts me. Nothing of my former mind seems to have remained except a heightened emotiveness which satisfies itself in the sixty-mile-an-hour pathos of some cinematograph.'[27]

John Huston was born in a small industrial town, Nevada, in south-western Missouri, a world far removed from Dublin, Trieste, Rome, Paris and Zurich, the cities that informed Joyce's life. Huston's *The Dead* would be completed eighty years after Joyce finished his story. How the world changed during those eighty years can be described, in no small part, as the arrival of speed, haste, accelerated time, the very quality of rapid sensation attributed by Joyce to cinema itself: its sixty-mile-an-hour pathos. Huston, whose life took its shape from the cinema industry and from cinema's fantastic acceleration of time and narrative, was sensitive to the difference between those cinematic conventions of speed and the demands of Joyce's uneventful, complex fiction: 'This one is like lacework,' Huston commented about the demands of directing *The Dead*. The structure of Joyce's story, he noticed, was in contrast 'to the forward direction of most films'. Referring to the central scene, the shared meal in the dining-room with all its small mishaps, he added, 'The biggest piece of action is trying to pass the port.'[28]

That is a small exaggeration. James Joyce's 'The Dead' is, among other things, a ghost story. A corpse rises from the dead and overwhelms Gretta and Gabriel Conroy as they leave the Misses Morkan's party and arrive at the Gresham Hotel. In the story it is the early hours of the morning when the party ends. In the film it is still night. In both story and film, windows mark the separation of light from dark, of inside from outside. Michael Furey had thrown gravel at young Gretta's window on a winter's night in Galway. She had heard a noise and looked to find him outside. Years later in a Dublin hotel room, she tells her husband Gabriel about that event in her past and about the young man's death. She falls asleep. The sound against the glass returns, and Gabriel hears it. 'A few light taps upon the pane made him turn to the window.' The reader believes the taps may be snowfall, although snow makes little or no noise when it falls. Nevertheless, the snow falling and the ghostly taps against the window cause Gabriel to imagine, as in a modulation of gothic fictions, 'the form of a young man standing under a dripping tree'.

The film, deliberately, does not show us on screen this ghost at the centre of Joyce's story. One of Huston's most reticent acts of fidelity to Joyce's 'The Dead' is that he allows it to remain a story in which the most powerful character, Michael Furey, does not put in an appearance. Huston could have inserted a flashback that would give material reality to Gretta's reminiscence. Indeed Tony Huston, John's son and the author of the screenplay, suggested that one solution to the difficulties of ending the film might be the insertion of flashbacks that would allow viewers to see at least visual suggestions of Michael Furey beneath a dripping tree.[29] That was not done and *The Dead* remains, as a film, consistent with this essential structure of the text from which it derives. Joyce had learned from Anatole France how a story could be constructed around a character who is not present. France had done as much throughout a narrative in which Pontius Pilate, without once mentioning Jesus of Nazareth, remembers his period of office as 'The Procurator of Judaea'. When Jesus is named to Pilate at the end of the story, Pilate cannot recall him. Charles Stewart Parnell serves a similar function in Joyce's 'Ivy Day in the Committee Room', and Michael Furey does so in 'The Dead'.[30] Huston, by refusing a flashback into the scenes of Gretta's early life, maintains in his film this convention of an absent centre upon which the story depends.

Although there is some dramatic action in Joyce's story, Huston was right to compare it to lacework. The story has a delicate spatial form and a complex verbal texture that mitigate its slow temporal rhythms. In the complex verbal texture of Joyce's story, the vast hosts of the dead take many shapes. There is a web of allusions to Irish political history: the victory of William of Orange at the Battle of Aughrim; the Back Lane Parliament, called in 1792 in answer to the revolution in France; the United Irishmen's password 'Is Ivers of Carlow come?' There is a web of allusions also to earlier literature: Homer's *Iliad* and its snowfalls (Book XII); Shakespeare's ghost story *Hamlet*, with Ophelia's repetition of 'Good night' (IV.v); Emily Brontë's gothic novel *Wuthering Heights*, with its ghost at the window; George Moore's novel *Vain Fortune*, with its final hotel bedroom scene of remorse for the suicide of a spouse's lover; Thomas Moore's *Irish Melodies*, in particular the song 'O, Ye Dead', about the snowbound corpses who demand new life; Walt Whitman's 'A Song for Occupations' and 'Song of Myself', with their competing sense of obligation to history; Lady Gregory's and W. B. Yeats's play *Cathleen Ni Houlihan*, with its exultation in death as a repeated sacrifice to the 'Sovranty of Ireland'.

Joyce's story has intertextual relationships also with an Irish story far earlier than *Cathleen Ni Houlihan*: the old Irish saga, *Togail Bruidhne Dá Derga* (The Destruction of Da Derga's Hostel), in which a blameless King Conaire breaks taboos that have been laid upon him and is defeated. Threefold patterns inform the saga (Conaire's three foster brothers, his nine taboos, his nine nights away from Tara, the three red horsemen). Joyce's doubtful hero is defeated three times and under three different forms of his name: first, as Mr 'Con-o-roy' by Lily, who pronounces his surname with an extra syllable and thus identifies him with the hero of the saga; second, as 'G. C.' by Miss Ivors, who identifies him by his published initials in the *Daily Express*; and third, as 'Gabriel' by Gretta. Joyce's complex verbal text plays variations upon political and literary narratives that he wrote into 'The Dead'. Indeed, these intertextual motifs are so flexible and layered that Paul Muldoon has placed 'The Dead' within the fantastic web of an alphabetic history of Irish fictions, as the text to which all threads lead.[31]

The presence in Joyce's story of corpses or ghosts from the past should not obscure the story's atmosphere and milieu that made it recognizable to and contemporary with its first generation of readers. At the time of its composition during 1907 and of its first publication in 1914, 'The Dead' was a story about inhabitants of a city who were themselves contemporaries of Joyce and of those for whom he was writing. It was the last story to be added to the collection entitled *Dubliners*. Placed as a conclusion to those fourteen bleak tales, 'The Dead' altered the balance and meaning of Joyce's collection of stories. Joyce had famously admitted to his brother Stanislaus in 1906 that, 'Sometimes thinking of Ireland it seems to me that I have been unnecessarily harsh. I have reproduced (in *Dubliners* at least) none of the attraction of the city.' The addition of 'The Dead', completed a year later, made some deliberate amendments and acknowledged in Joyce's fiction for the first time what he affectionately described as the city's 'ingenuous insularity and hospitality'.[32] This final story exhibits many differences from the other stories of *Dubliners*. Two differences most vividly set it apart: food at its centre and style at its end. Food, in 'The Dead', is a custom of civility: it is plentiful, varied, ceremonious and generously shared. And the style of the final paragraphs of this story embodies a register of conscious (perhaps self-conscious) lyric ideality that, however we choose to interpret its status and value, is not to be found elsewhere in the relatively limited heteroglossia of *Dubliners*.

The characters at the dinner table of 'The Dead' are Joyce's contemporaries and early contemporaries. They are, for the most part, based upon Joyce's extended family and their friends. Every year the Joyce family would attend a party at his great aunts' house, 15 Usher's Island, on Dublin's quays: parents, children, cousins and acquaintances. Joyce's father would carve the goose and give the after-dinner speech.[33] In the story, these contemporaries, some older and some younger, are in the habit of talking about the past and of idealizing the dead. They regret, in varieties of comfort and discomfort, the loss of a past they judge to be more vivid and more full of life than the present. Joyce's story is about a diverse group of people who are, to different degrees, haunted by a past that is lost. The story, therefore, is about nostalgia. But the narrative and thematic pattern of recollection, celebrated and regretted, should not mislead us into thinking that the story is, of itself, nostalgic. On its first appearance, the story was unambiguously modern for its readers: perhaps a little 'queer' and 'old-fashioned', as a reviewer in the *New Statesman* found it to be, but the manners of a provincial city have always appeared a little *passé* to the metropolis.[34]

Readers today, by contrast, encounter 'The Dead' as a period piece, as if the story is nostalgic in its very form. For readers now 'The Dead' is not simply a representation of characters who feel nostalgic about the past. Nostalgia for today's belated readers is doubled. There is a sense that the story recalls a lost world – Dublin at the turn of the century – and in that lost world the story's characters reduplicate 'our' nostalgia: we, no less than they, appear to be in the business of recalling lost worlds. That twofold nostalgia, a nostalgia that emerges during the eighty years elapsing between the story's composition and its cinematic version, played a decisive part in the direction, casting, lighting, design, production, advertising and reception of John Huston's film *The Dead*, both in Ireland and internationally.

One of the primary events in that eighty years, as we have noticed, is the popular diffusion of cinema itself. The world of 1987 is a world shaped by cinema in a way that the world of 1904 had not been. Indeed, Joyce's proposal to four Triestine businessmen, that together they open the Volta cinema in Dublin in 1909, began with his seductive declaration: 'I know a city of 500,000 inhabitants where there is not a single cinema.'[35] The Dublin of 'The Dead' is a city of concert halls and theatres, not of cinemas. The Volta failed in its first year, but, by the time Huston came to make 'The Dead' into a movie, Dublin had established a record of more cinema seats per one thousand inhabitants than any European city other than Prague.

We can allow that cinema here stands for, not only the might of film industries and their omnipresence in modern consciousness, not only the acceleration of the speed of social life and the abbreviation of its narrative forms, but also for the substitution throughout the length of the twentieth century of virtual performance for live performance. Cinema, television, recorded music, mechanical and electronic reproductions of all kinds now constitute an idea of performance unimaginable in the drawing-room world of the Misses Morkan or in the surprise and attention shown by Gretta Conroy to the casual singing of a song that she half remembers, and of which she has forgotten the title. Indeed Joyce's story can be read now as the testimony by one contemporary witness to a popular urban culture of live performance on the eve of its rapid decline.

Consider, for example, how Joyce's dinner-table exchanges about the merits of different tenors and contraltos are referenced by live performance. Where recordings were unavailable, memory vitally depended upon 'being there'. Mary Jane would 'give anything to hear Caruso sing'. In the absence of aural and visual recordings, memory and word of mouth constituted the limits of evidence. The old had the edge on the young. Aunt Kate's experience and range of reference goes back in time, further even than those of Mr Browne: she prefers the pure English tenor Parkinson, whom she heard when he was in his prime – 'But I suppose none of you ever heard of him.' Mr Browne has heard of Parkinson, but has never heard him sing. Young Bartell D'Arcy has not heard of him at all. For readers today, Joyce's story testifies to quite specific interactions of memory and event that now, in a media and hi-fi world of simulacra and virtual performance, appear irretrievably lost. It is largely for this reason that 'The Dead' appears to be a 'period piece'. The story as filmed seems now to be a warm recollection of a lost urban world, a world before the arrival of cinema. It is a world of domestic courtesies, of concert-going and of private parties that themselves are intimate forms of concert-giving: Aunt Julia sang; Mary Jane played; and Bartell D'Arcy too. Live performances of such a kind are rare in the modern metropolis. The fictional participants within the story are of an age and time (let us call it 1904) that ensures for the audiences of Huston's film one key fact: not only these characters but also their habits of life are dead, and we may wish in our nostalgia that it were not so.

In 1987, therefore, *The Dead* fulfilled exactly the definition of cinema that Christian Metz had enunciated in 1985 when contrasting the idea of cinema with that of photography. In particular Metz was commenting on Roland Barthes' claim, in *Camera Lucida*, that photography is tied to death. Metz found here an opportunity to

Plate 7.

defend film against photography. 'Film', Metz argued, 'gives back to the dead a semblance of life, a fragile semblance, but one immediately strengthened by the wishful thinking of the viewer'. The photograph, therefore, becomes the direct opposite of cinema, as each reproduces its subject. Film raises the dead, gives the dead life. A photograph, by contrast, sentences the living to death, and functions always as a *memento mori*. A photograph of the dead, 'by virtue of the objective suggestion of its signifier (stillness, again), maintains the memory of the dead *as being dead*'.[36] Film denies this irremediable death of the past which the still photograph accepts.

Given this distinction between film and photograph, the one a ghostly animation of the dead, the other a *memento mori*, we can provide some analysis of the way in which Huston's film uses photographs. At that point in the film when Aunt Julia sings 'Arrayed for the Bridal', the camera moves away from her performance and ascends the stairs to her bedroom, a bedroom identified by its mementos of the past and in particular by its framed sepia photographs of her family. That filming of framed photographs, along with the use of apparently still shots, at the end of the film, of graves, crosses and snow-covered trees, has specific consequences for the viewer. The filming of photographs ensures that the movie defines two different time-scales of death: one, the dead that it brings to life (whether Aunt Julia, Mr Browne or Gretta Conroy) who can enjoy the party, sing and talk; two, the dead whom these living dead remember and regret – that is, the irremediably dead, those whose voices are only a memory, such as Michael Furey, or old Parkinson, or poor Georgina Burns, who died young. Gabriel's anticipation of Aunt Julia's death, which is inserted as a flash-forward at the end of Huston's film, is the single instance of an inevitable merging of these two communities of death.

Huston's film aesthetic largely coheres with Metz's definition of cinema. Huston is preoccupied by the interplay between the flickering ghosts we see on the screen and our nostalgic wish to see those ghosts alive. Huston is especially aware, as also is Metz, of film's capacity to project the viewer's desires onto the screen:

> There are many things inherent in the medium that work for you; the whole immediacy of the experience, and the subjectivity of the emotions that can derive from a good film. The ideal film, it seems to me, is when it's as though the projector were behind the beholder's eyes, and he throws onto the screen that which he *wants* to see.[37]

Given the critical fame of James Joyce and of his story, one of the things viewers *wanted* was fidelity: to see on screen a faithful transcription of 'The Dead' into picture-book form. Huston continually represents his method as director in terms of fidelity, clarity, simplicity, unselfconsciousness. In defence of his conviction that 'everything technical is only a method to make the idea into clear form', Huston argued that:

There are maybe half a dozen directors who really know
their camera – how to move their camera. It's a pity that
critics often do not appreciate this. On the one hand I think
it's OK that audiences should not be aware of this. In fact,
when the camera is in motion, in the best-directed scenes,
the audience should not be aware of what the camera is
doing. They should be following the action and the road of
the idea so closely, that they shouldn't be aware of what's
going on technically.[38]

Fidelity, a most unJoycean value, became a requirement of the film's
legitimacy even before the cameras began to roll. Previews of the film
anticipated the fidelity of film to story and often cited Huston's and
the film's Irishness as evidence that such an expectation would be met.
For example, Ronan Farren, writing in the *Sunday Independent* in 1986
about the casting of the film, and in particular the choice of Donal
McCann to play opposite Anjelica Huston, wrote:

Veteran director John Huston, who had originally intended
to make the film here [in Ireland], has written the screenplay
himself and is assembling a strong Irish and Irish-American
cast for his long-cherished project. [Geraldine Fitzgerald
will play] one of the elderly aunts, a part originally intended
for the late Siobhan McKenna.[39]

Farren added a comment from Ingrid Craigie, another Irish actress
cast in the forthcoming film: Huston, she reminded us, 'lived in Co.
Galway for over ten years and his daughter Anjelica was mainly
educated in Ireland'.

During the period of post-production, before the film's release, the
actress Maria McDermottroe (Molly Ivors) summarized a similar
view about the fidelity of the film and the film-making process to the
story's place and time:

> The Irish and the Irish-American people are true
> professionals . . . The crew behind the cameras included
> Josie MacAvin, the Irishwoman who won an Oscar for her
> set-dressing on *Out of Africa*, and a woman called Dorothy
> Jeakins on costumes, who has a complete love for Ireland.
> She had met Maud Gonne when she was younger and was
> not unlike Maud Gonne herself.[40]

Fred Murphy, Director of Photography, anticipated the release of *The Dead* by recalling how period atmosphere was the most important topic of conversation between himself and Huston during the planning stages of the lighting for the film set:

> John gave me a description of Ireland at the time. Not the
> way Ireland *looked*, but the way the people in this story felt
> and the way their environment should feel. John speaks very
> abstractly, but he was interested in the picture having a kind
> of turn-of-the-century glow.[41]

Press information from the production company also anticipated the fidelity of the film to the aura of the story. When money had first been raised to make *The Dead*, the Production Manager, Tom Shaw, had been of the view that the film could be shot anywhere, since 'the whole goddamn thing takes place in a house'. Huston had disagreed. 'I don't want to ever make that movie unless it can be made in Ireland,' he told Shaw.[42] However, Huston's failing health ensured that the film be made on a set in the United States. Tony Huston, author of the screenplay, recalls that exact measurements were taken of the house on Usher's Island and precise use was made of Joyce's descriptions of the rooms. He recalls that genuine Victorian objects, not fake copies, decorated the rooms: the 'spirit' of the objects matter, he argued, and therefore he had scoured local 'swap-me' stores for authentic items.[43] Press information from Vestron Pictures and Liffey

Films confronted the location problem and overcame it with some extraordinary hyperbole:

> Although set in Dublin . . . production of The Dead was mounted in an industrial warehouse in Valencia, California, a desert town located just north of Los Angeles. The house in which Joyce set his story, as well as the Quay of the river Liffey across from the house, were reconstructed in such painstaking detail that all the props and fixtures were flown in from Ireland . . . Featured in the cast were Huston's daughter, Anjelica Huston, who grew up in Ireland . . . and other actors from Dublin's famed Abbey and Gate Theatres, including Kate O'Toole, daughter of Peter O'Toole.[44]

Such pre-emptive strikes in favour of the fidelity of a film of 'The Dead' by Huston were not merely journalistic Irish sentiment or the well-marketed nostalgia of a press release. The ideal of conformity between a work of narrative fiction and its cinematic version has underpinned a considerable amount of recent critical thinking about relations between literature and film in the second half of the twentieth century. John Orr, for example, in a collection of essays published in 1992 under the title *Cinema and Fiction: New Modes of Adapting, 1950–1990*, argues that:

> The picture-book is at its best when film and text are part of the same culture, part of the same age, yet also when some time has elapsed between book and film, when the picture-book is also a retrospective rendering of the text.[45]

As evidence, he cites the success of Visconti's version (1964) of Lampedusa's *The Leopard* (1938), Bertolucci's version (1969) of Moravia's *The Conformist* (1952) and Orson Welles' version (1960) of Kafka's *The Trial* (1912). All these instances provide persuasive analogies with the 'retrospective rendering of the text' in Huston's *The Dead*.

Writing in *Sight and Sound*, immediately after the release of Huston's film, Tim Pulleine aligned the fidelity of *The Dead* with the practice of earlier Huston adaptations. The film exemplified a:

> continuation – in the event, a culmination – of one of its maker's abiding concerns: 'I try to be as faithful as I can to the material I have chosen to film.' We are in Dublin at the start of the new century. It is Twelfth Night, the Feast of the Epiphany, and sundry friends and relatives are arriving for the annual party given by the elderly Miss Morkans, retired maiden ladies. Here is Dublin's middle-class society – the mirror of Joyce's Ireland – contained by a somewhat self-conscious complacency.[46]

So also wrote Denis Donoghue in the *New York Review of Books*: 'The film', he declared, 'is superb in the most comprehensive regard: it respects its origin'.[47]

Of John Huston's thirty-seven feature films, thirty-four are adaptations of novels, stories, or plays. In all cases, Huston had favoured the option of fidelity to a text. The first author he adapted, for his directorial debut, was Dashiell Hammett. The last was Joyce. In between these two extremes he adapted, amongst many others, B. Traven, Stephen Crane, C. S. Forester, Herman Melville, Tennessee Williams, Flannery O'Connor, Carson McCullers and Malcolm Lowry. When Huston came to summarize the process of adaptation he preferred, his arguments hinged upon fidelity and authenticity of interpretation: 'It's the fascination that I feel for the original that makes me want to make it into a film,' he insisted in a celebrated interview with Gideon Bachmann. 'Very often it's something I read 25 or 30 years ago, or when I was a child.'[48] It was James Agee who first celebrated Huston's film-making, in a *Life* magazine panegyric of 1950, and Agee identified fidelity to a text as the hallmark of Huston's chameleon-like directorial style: 'Each of Huston's pictures has a visual tone and style of its own,' wrote Agee, 'dictated to his camera by the story's essential content and spirit.'[49] Huston is a stylist precisely because he has no personal style.

The dictation of the original story to its cinematic version is not the only fate that Joyce's 'The Dead' could have anticipated. James Naremore has written of how Huston does indeed offer:

> a sensitive and unfailingly intelligent translation of Joyce into visual and dramatic form. Most of the dialogue in his film is taken directly from the original text, and whenever new speeches are invented . . . it is difficult to detect where Joyce's words leave off and the adaptation begins. The cast of largely Irish actors inhabits its various roles with absolute conviction and the *mise-en-scène* conveys an appropriate mixture of down-at-heels gentility and impending death.

And yet, Naremore modifies his praise for Huston's film with a critical reserve about its formal and aesthetic limitations: the total

Plate 8.

effect of the Huston film, he argues, is 'almost Dickensian'. To translate Joyce faithfully into another medium is in conflict with the modernist, disruptive and ironic use of previous narratives, practised in all Joycean texts, not least in 'The Dead' itself. Hence, Naremore concludes:

> Ironically, any effort at rendering Joyce in another medium entails a series of assumptions and procedures that are fundamentally unJoycean . . . a reverend adaptation continually runs the risk of becoming just the sort of middlebrow artefact that Joyce had quietly satirized throughout his story.[50]

The lapse of time between story and film, the cultural integrity of the film's *mise-en-scène*, the faithfulness of screenplay to the letter of the text, the authenticity of the Irishness of the film's casting and filmic texture, all these are constitutive of the relationship between the production of Huston's film and its reception. However, things could have been otherwise. And at least one other film version of 'The Dead' diverges spectacularly from the principle of identity between version and origin, between film and text, which is invoked not only by Huston, but also by the actors, producers and reviewers of *The Dead*.

4

THE ALIENATION OF THE DEAD

In 1953 Roberto Rossellini filmed *Voyage to Italy*. It is a film set in Sicily after World War II. The action focuses upon an English married couple, played by Ingrid Bergman and George Sanders,

Plate 9.

whose eight-year marriage is under stress as they combine a southern holiday with the sale of a villa left to them by her dead Uncle Homer. The couple's names are Mr and Mrs Joyce, Katherine and Alex. Consider the following transcript of the moment of crisis that occurs midway through Rossellini's film; Mr and Mrs Joyce are sitting on the sun-drenched terrace of Uncle Homer's villa.

KATHERINE: Do you remember poor Charles?

ALEX: Charles who?

KATHERINE: Charles Lewington.

ALEX: Lewington?

KATHERINE: He died two years ago.

ALEX: Oh, and you just heard about it.

KATHERINE: No, I knew the day after his death. Two years ago.

ALEX: Lewington. I don't seem to be able to remember the fellow. Where did we meet him?

KATHERINE: At the Hooper-Smiths.

ALEX: Was he a lawyer?

KATHERINE: No, he was a poet. He was thin, tall, pale, so pale and spiritual. He was stationed here in Italy during the war. Right here as a matter of fact.

ALEX: Oh, yes I think I remember him. He was at one of Arthur's concerts. He had a fit of coughing and had to leave the auditorium.

KATHERINE: Yes he was very ill. Something he caught during the war.

ALEX: You know, that young man started me thinking about something.

KATHERINE: About what?

ALEX: That you can learn more from the way a man coughs than from the way he speaks.

KATHERINE: What did Charles' cough tell you?

ALEX: That he was a fool.

KATHERINE: He was not a fool. He was a poet.

ALEX: What's the difference?

KATHERINE: Charles wrote some wonderful poems.

ALEX: I must get one of his books.

KATHERINE: Well, you won't find any. He was too young to have any of his books published.

ALEX: Then how did you know about them?

KATHERINE: He read them to me. I even copied some. 'Temple of the spirit, / No longer bodies but pure ascetic images, / Compared to which mere thought seems flesh, / Heavy, dim.' He wrote them here in Italy while he was in the war.

ALEX: I never knew you were such great friends.

KATHERINE: Oh, I knew him before I met you.

ALEX: Were you in love with him?

KATHERINE: No, but we got on terribly well together. I saw a great deal of him at Copping Farm. Then he got desperately ill. I couldn't even visit him. For almost a year I didn't see him. Then, on the eve of our wedding, the night before I left for London, I was packing my bags, when I heard the sound of pebbles on the window. The rain was so heavy, I couldn't see anyone outside. So I ran out into the garden, just as I was, and there he was. He was shivering with cold. He was so strange and romantic. Maybe he wanted to prove to me that, in spite of the high fever, he had braved the rain to see me. Or maybe he wanted to die.

ALEX: How very poetic. Much more poetic than his verses.[51]

Rossellini's *Voyage to Italy* returns 'The Dead' to the country where the story had been composed, and not to the Ireland that is its subject.

The film bears a fascinating relationship to Joyce's story, because that relationship is indirect. Rossellini does not retell the story as a classic, as an original to which he must be true. His dependence upon Joyce's text is marked by the central quotation and misquotation of Gretta's recollection of Michael Furey, of the pebbles or gravel against the window, of the rain blinding her view of the outside, of her running downstairs and out to the garden 'as I was'. There are other momentary allusions, such as Alex's observation that he is 'sick of this country, sick of it', a remark that echoes and inverts Gabriel's outburst to Miss Ivors. For it is his own country that Gabriel is sick of, whereas Alex is sick of Italy, and is eager to get back to his own home and work in England. *Voyage to Italy* is not in any sense an imitation of 'The Dead', but its narrative dynamic is the same as that identified by Stanislaus Joyce when he wrote of how,

> In 'The Dead' the two polar attitudes of men towards women, that of the lover and that of the husband, are presented compassionately. It is not the eternal triangle of falsity and deception. The two men at different times in the woman's life have loved her with equal sincerity each in his way, and there is no guile in the woman. But one love is the enemy of the other, and the dead lover's romantic passion, outliving his mortal flesh, is still dominant in the woman's heart.[52]

In spite of all the differences, then, the central dilemma of Rossellini's movie is entirely congruent with Joyce's story, and the screenplay, written in collaboration with Vitaliano Brancati, recalls more than the phrasing of Gretta's memory of Michael Furey. In both Joyce and Rossellini we find a couple who are married but who do not know each other well, and we witness them arriving at a momentary realization of their predicament through memories of the dead (Plate 9). East and West in Joyce's story become North and South in Rossellini. Sicily is to London in Rossellini's film as Galway is to Dublin in 'The Dead'. Both Joyce and Rossellini immerse their narratives in remembrances and forge equations between death, emotional intensity and compassion. In Joyce's story, for example, there are all those dead generations remembered in Gabriel's after-dinner speech, the compassion for others shown by the monks of Mount Melleray when each night they anticipate their own deaths, and the pity for the singer Georgina Burns. In *Voyage to Italy* there are the catacombs, and Pompeii, and dead Uncle Homer, and also (reminiscent of Mr Browne's astonishment at the behaviour of the monks of Mount Melleray) Katherine Joyce's astonishment at the Sicilians' compassion for the dead. This compassion is most vividly demonstrated in her exchange with the caretaker's wife, Natalia, at the villa before they visit the catacombs. Their visit centres upon a necropolis that Natalia explains to Katherine:

NATALIA: Where they gather skeletons from ancient cemeteries.

KATHERINE: Sounds very dismal.

NATALIA: Dismal? Quite the contrary. These are skeletons of people who died two or three or even four hundred years ago. Can you imagine?

KATHERINE: I don't think it sounds very amusing.

NATALIA: But that's because you've never been to the place. You wouldn't believe it because a few people go there. There are *many* people who have chosen a skeleton, assembled it properly, take care of it lovingly, bring fresh flowers every so often, and keep a light in front of it.

KATHERINE: But what's the meaning of all that?

NATALIA: Oh, it's pity, I guess. These poor dead are abandoned and alone, they have no one to look after them, no one to pray for them.

Plate 10.

KATHERINE: But I don't understand. I just can't understand.
NATALIA: I know. It is difficult to understand, but you will see
for yourself.

Voyage to Italy places the figure of Katherine at an ironic distance (Plate 10). Her husband mocks her and the camera refuses to submit her to the idealization that underlies almost all readings of Gretta in Joyce's 'The Dead'. John Huston's version, as enacted by Anjelica Huston, corresponds with an idealization of Gretta which remains an assumption of humanist and postcolonial readings of 'The Dead', and is qualified only by certain feminist criticism. Rossellini deconstructs Joyce's Gretta by means of the figure of Katherine, who is in many scenes foolish, petulant and at a loss (Plate 11). In *Voyage to Italy*, both wife and husband are the subject of humorous, compassionate and satiric observation (Plate 12).

Plate 11.

There is, in Rossellini's version of the couple's dilemma, a modernist refusal to allow the viewer to take sides. Indeed, the romantic attachment of Gretta to Michael Furey here becomes the subject of an ironic displacement: Katherine's reverence for the dead Charles is less and less persuasive. She herself discovers that his verses, which she had learned by heart ('Temple of the spirit / No longer bodies'), are a graceful misunderstanding of the gross bodily statues and skeletons with which Sicily confronts her. It is their immodesty that shocks her. 'Poor Charles', she admits to Alex, 'he had a way all his own of seeing things.' So, too, the reconciliation between wife and husband at the conclusion of *Voyage to Italy* is a momentary and not a transcendent incident. The embrace of Katherine and Alex is hedged about with cautious words, and the camera includes in a close shot of their desperate embrace the indifferent faces in the crowd around them (Plate 13), and then moves away to the casual business of

Plate 12.

Plate 13.

townspeople and police officers. The film is extraordinarily inconsequential, The flatness of its ending is memorable and its use of *temps mort* remorseless. For these reasons, the film was as unsuccessful when released in Italy as it was celebrated in France, where it came to be seen as a precursor of the *nouvelle vague*. In 1961 the French critic Pierre Marcabru discovered in *Voyage to Italy* a new cinema of the non-event: 'In the immobile and the insignificant is the very power of life.'[53]

Rossellini's *Voyage to Italy*, therefore, is a profoundly Joycean text, both in its modernism and in its playing fast and loose with Joyce's own story. Indeed, Rossellini's film also plays fast and loose with Gertrude Stein's novel *Duo* (1934), another account of the 'happily married' couple whose marriage is falling apart under the pressure of a previous love. Rossellini's failure to buy the rights of the Stein novel may be one reason why he merges its fiction with that of Joyce's 'The

Dead'.[54] Such humour, deconstructive irony and refusal of fidelity to any one text are common to Joyce's 'The Dead' and to *Voyage to Italy*. Indeed, an incidental value of Rossellini's film may be to encourage readers to return to 'The Dead' with a more wilful eye to interpretation of the Gretta/Michael Furey axis: its latent necrophilia, its repetition in a higher key of a reverence for the dead past that permeates all moments and characters in Joyce's story.

Rossellini's version of 'The Dead' is untroubled by the 'Irishness' of the story. Instead, Rossellini follows through on possibilities that had first been noticed by Ezra Pound in one of the earliest reviews of *Dubliners*:

> It is surprising that Mr Joyce is Irish. One is so tired of the Irish or 'Celtic' imagination (or 'phantasy' as I think they now call it) flopping about. Mr Joyce does not flop about. He defines. He is not an institution for the promotion of Irish peasant industries . . . He gives us things as they are, not only for Dublin, but for every city. Erase the local names and a few specifically local allusions, and a few historic events of the past, and substitute a few different local names, allusions and events, and these stories could be retold of any town. . . Roughly speaking, Irish literature has gone through three phases in our time, the shamrock period, the dove-grey period, and the Kiltartan period. I think there is a new phase in the works of Mr Joyce. He writes as a contemporary of continental writers.'[55]

John Huston's film of 'The Dead' is, by contrast with that of Rossellini, unJoycean in its formal procedures precisely because it is faithful to the Irish milieu of Joyce's text. Such faithfulness is not lessened by the omissions and additions that viewers can detect in Huston's rewriting of the story for the cinema. Part of the fascination and authority of Huston's film can be discovered in the interplay between, on the one hand, his fidelity to the text and, on the other, the transformations imposed on him by a lapse of eighty years and by the medium of film itself. It is an irony of his intention to be faithful that Huston must alter so much in the text to which he wishes to be true.

Few critics have noted the many important ways in which Huston's film diverges from Joyce's story. Lesley Brill, in his *John Huston's Filmmaking* (1997), does explore these divergences. He divides Huston's *oeuvre* between adaptations that are strictly faithful to an original text and those that are not. He observes that *The Dead* falls into the group of adaptations that substantially diverge from the original text. That group includes the movie versions of *Moby Dick* and *Under the Volcano*. The group of strictly faithful adaptations is typified by *The Maltese Falcon* and *Reflections in a Golden Eye*.[56] A list of Huston's divergences from Joyce can be briefly itemized: Huston excises scenes from 'The Dead'; he adds scenes; he adds one important character to the guest list and deletes almost all the younger guests; he lengthens the middle and he shortens the end; he has Molly Ivors wink at Gabriel; he has Gabriel distinctly hear the song that Gretta listens to on the stairs; he moves the story of Johnny the horse from the hallway of the house to the intimacy of the carriage; he inserts montage effects and moments of what we might call 'explanatory' dialogue; he repositions points of view and avails of proxemic distance to establish sympathy; he explicitly dates the events in the film to the night of 6 January 1904.[57]

Such divergences should prompt us to assess John Huston's *The Dead* as an independent work of cinema, as one among his thirty-four adaptations of classic and minor writers, and finally as the extraordinary last testament of an international film-maker who established his own identity by a chameleon-like adaptability to texts by diverse hands. We can dramatically bring that diversity to mind simply by naming Huston's last four movies: *Annie* (1982), *Under the Volcano* (1984),

Prizzi's Honor (1985), *The Dead* (1987). When interviewed on the set of his movie *The Bible* in Rome in 1965, Huston asserted not immodestly: 'I try to be as faithful to the original material as I can. This applies equally to Melville as it applies to *The Bible*.' However, he immediately added a paradoxical assertion that he has something coherent to say in his films, even if almost all of them rewrite stories told by others. It is the same paradox applied to a lifetime's work that Walter Benjamin had applied to the ideal text: a work that is constituted wholly of quotations. In Huston's more informal phrasing: 'You could draw a portrait of a mind through that mind's preferences.'[58]

Let us return to our first observation. John Huston was born in Nevada, Missouri, in 1906. Some eighty years later he would make a film based on a story written by a young Europeanized Irishman, James Joyce. Huston and Joyce are separated not only by those eighty years, but by the spectacular fact that their lives could scarcely have been more different: the one living a bookish, private life in the world of words, the other living a flamboyant public life in the business of pictures. The world changed immeasurably during those eighty years. Such cultural distance and difference ensure that Huston could not be perfectly faithful to Joyce even if he wanted to be.

The question then presents itself: what can we learn from a closer inspection of Huston's necessary infidelities to Joyce? The film is a powerful misreading of the story. By this I do not only mean that the film is formally unfaithful to the aesthetic upon which the story depends, precisely because it pretends to be faithful to its milieu and its tone. Rather, I mean that the film misreads the story powerfully because it alters it almost invisibly: the viewer is often persuaded that the film has not changed the story at all, because Huston's adaptation so tactfully satisfies the viewer's expectations. That is to say, the film changes the story persuasively because, given a lapse of eighty years, it does so unobtrusively.

If we read against the grain of the film and dramatize its misreading of the story, we can learn something of our own distance from Joyce's story. We can measure the lapse of eighty years in ways that are specific to both story and film: in those eighty years had occurred transforming events to which the story is blind but the film more or less clear-sighted. In order to clarify our analysis, we shall limit these events to four: the realization of an Irish national narrative of sovereign independence; the development of a classic Hollywood narrative style; the establishment of John Huston's *oeuvre*; the cultivation of a James Joyce critical industry.

Each of these four events can be matched by at least one moment of flagrant infidelity in the film. Such moments are memorable: they occur on the upper landing; in the drawing-room; in the Misses Morkan's bathroom; in the hotel bedroom. Each episode can illustrate a different aspect of the dynamic play of interpretation that preoccupies readers of the story and viewers of the film, whether their commitment is to the work of Joyce, to that of Huston, or to both.

5

ON THE LANDING:
THE IRISH NATIONAL NARRATIVE

On the landing between two flights of stairs, Gretta and Mary Jane meet Molly Ivors descending from the floor above. The screenplay reads as follows:

> MARY JANE: But you can't leave before supper.
> *Gabriel comes through to join them.*
> MOLLY IVORS: I'm not in the least hungry, I assure you.
> GRETTA: But only for ten minutes, Molly, that won't delay you.
> MARY JANE: To take a pick itself after all your dancing.
> MOLLY IVORS: I really can't.
> *Gabriel steps forward.*
> GABRIEL: If you really are obliged to go, I'd be happy to see you home.
> MOLLY IVORS: I'm not going home. I'm off to a meeting.
> GABRIEL: Oh, what kind of a meeting?
> MOLLY IVORS: A union one at Liberty Hall. James Connolly's speaking.
> GABRIEL (suspiciously): You mean a Republican meeting.
> MARY JANE: Sure you'll be the only woman there.
> MOLLY IVORS: It won't be the first time. Well good-night all. Beannacht libh.
> *With a laugh she runs down the staircase as Gabriel and Gretta look at each other and shrug.*[59]

The unfaithfulness to the text here appears to be slight, but its consequences are enormous, and deeply illuminating about Joyce's story and its necessary blindness about the future. In Joyce's story, Miss Ivors leaves the party at the same moment and in much the same manner as in Huston's film. However, in the story she has nowhere to go except, perhaps, home. In the film, on the other hand, she leaves the party and knows where she is going. She has acquired a historical destiny: she is striding towards the Easter Rising of 1916, towards the death of James Connolly, a leader of that rebellion, a rebellion that, according to a national narrative of self-determination, led directly to Irish independence from England. But Joyce's story tells a different story, a story blind to what now appears to be the historical destiny of Ireland. Joyce's text tells the story of a Catholic middle class that has no inkling of violent rebellion, a Catholic middle class of small ambitions which is almost indifferent to a fiction that will become in hindsight the national narrative of Ireland.[60]

Viewers of the film, who remember that Miss Ivors did not originally leave the party with such an exciting motive, return to Joyce's story with a new awareness. They become aware perhaps for the first time of a social formation, which the future almost erased but which is represented in Joyce's story: an Irish Catholic middle class untroubled by the fact that Ireland is going nowhere except towards home, or, we might say, towards Home Rule. Sovereign independence from London is of no concern to the Misses Morkan and their guests, who, in Joyce's story, know nothing of a teleological nationalist narrative imposed on them by history and by Huston's film. In the film, Miss Ivors denies her maker, Joyce, and declares: 'I'm not going home. I'm off to a meeting.' For the audience of the film, therefore, her cultural nativism merges with a republican political future that is itself merged with her commitments to the labour movement and to feminism, a proleptic synthesis about which Joyce's story is necessarily unaware. Huston's film inserts into Joyce's story an Irish national narrative of self-determination that, within the eighty-year lapse of time between story and film, had become a founding assumption of the film's audiences. The addition of a censored mention of Parnell at the dinner table, imported from *A Portrait of the Artist as a Young Man*, offers a belated genealogy to the naming of James Connolly by Miss Ivors. The unobtrusiveness of these infidelities of film to text depends upon a shared acceptance of a grand, national narrative with which Joyce's micro-narrative, 'The Dead', had been blindly at odds.

The film here is consistent with many analytic misreadings of Joyce's story, not least those that propose their method to be New Historicism. For example, Michael Levenson offers a reading of Joyce's 'The Dead' that is oddly anachronistic and determinist. He reads a grand, national narrative back into the very structure of the story, its progression and its antitheses. He recognizes that the evening party, with its circulation of food and feeling,

> is colonial Ireland at its best – so 'The Dead' implies – and yet even at its best, it is decaying and fragile: the moments of collective self-affirmation, painfully achieved, bear signs of insupportable tension. Refusing to acknowledge the political provocations that circulate in their festive midst, content to surround themselves with the allure of art and literature, these colonial subjects manufacture a simulacrum of autonomy. Its hollowness is not only enforced by its reliance on *English* cultural tradition, neatly captured by the scene from *Romeo and Juliet* hanging on the wall, but emphatically by the inability to suppress a distinctly *Irish* provocation, first articulated by Miss Ivors and then embodied, in the story's climax, by Gretta Conroy.[61]

The implicit analogies of entropy ('decaying and fragile') and of an emptiness to be replaced by fullness ('colonial Ireland . . . Its hollowness' versus 'distinctly *Irish* . . . embodied, in the story's climax') depend upon a teleology supplied by hindsight. The antithesis of English and Irish cultural traditions is at odds with the party scene in which the guests discuss many European cultures, including that of England. The guests are no more dependent on English culture than was Shakespeare on the Italy of *Romeo and Juliet*'s Verona.[62] In identifying Miss Ivors' jibes at Gabriel with Gretta Conroy's final recollection of her past, Levenson equates the West of Ireland with that which is 'distinctly *Irish*' and justifies that equation by proposing an untroubled political continuity between Molly Ivors and Gretta Conroy. Finally, Levenson identifies the trope of the idealized West with the snow, which he emphasizes is, at the end of the story, 'all over Ireland'. His teleological analysis causes him to place the phrase 'all over Ireland' incorrectly in 'the story's last sentence' where it 'evokes the geography of a separate national identity. . . a unity that its colonial status has long blocked . . . a storm-driven Ireland flattened into the shape of a nation.'[63] Such a reading of 'The Dead', while proposing itself as historicist, is deeply anachronistic: as anachronistic as we, its belated readers, are tempted always to be, as anachronistic as Huston's film, with its historical determination of Miss Ivors' reasons for leaving the party. Viewers' expectations, after a lapse of eighty years, can be so easily satisfied, illusions about historical necessity so glibly assured.

6

IN THE DRAWING ROOM:
CLASSIC HOLLYWOOD NARRATIVE STYLE

James Joyce's 'The Dead' has an extraordinary narrative structure: it is almost 20,000 words in length, and of that total some 2,500 words cover what many readers consider to be the 'real' story, that is the story of Gretta and Michael Furey and its revelation to Gabriel. Readers have often agreed in their estimate of the value of these unequal portions: the first and longer portion, the Misses Morkan's party, has been read as introductory and more or less superficial in its subject matter; the second and shorter portion, the confessional scene in the Gresham Hotel bedroom, has been read as profoundly moving and epiphanic. Frank O'Connor, for example, noticed that:

> 'The Dead', Joyce's last story, is entirely different from all the others. It is also immensely more complicated, and it is not always easy to see what any particular episode represents, though it is only too easy to see that it represents something. The scene is the annual dance of the Misses Morkan, old music teachers on Usher's Island, and ostensibly it is no more than a report of what happened at it, except at the end, when Gabriel Conroy and his wife Gretta return to their hotel room. There she breaks down and tells him of a youthful and innocent love affair between herself and a boy of seventeen in Galway, who had caught his death of cold from standing under her bedroom window. But this final scene is irrelevant only in appearance, for in effect it is the real story, and everything that has led up to it has been simply an enormously expanded introduction, a series of themes all of which find their climax in the hotel bedroom.[64]

That such a structure makes considerable demands upon both author and reader had been noticed by Allen Tate when he defined how the story is divided into two unequal and apparently irrelevant portions, with little (except some symbolic mention of 'snow' and 'mortal' and 'perishing' cold) to link the second to the first: 'The [Furey] incident is one of great technical difficulty, for no preparation, in its own terms, was possible.' Kenneth Burke worked towards similar conclusions when he discovered a tripartite structure in 'The Dead': the first two stages (concerning Lily and the Misses Morkan's dinner party) exist in shared terms of 'everyday sociality', and the party itself, according to Burke, 'could be analysed almost as a catalogue of superficial socialities, each in its way slightly false or misfit'. The third stage, however, could not be more different in kind: 'the third section concerns initiation into a mystery. It is to take us beyond the realm of realism, as so conceived, into the realm of *ideality*'.[65]

Such an approach to reading 'The Dead' can continue beyond any reception of the film. The idea can remain that some profound reality arrives at the story's end to humiliate whatever has gone before. Luke Gibbons and others have slighted 'the routines and protocols of bourgeois decorum' during the long dinner party when 'Everyone goes through their paces but the night is stage-managed to the last. Party-pieces and the stilted conversation of role-playing are the most that can be achieved by way of self-expression.'[66] In this view, the West is awake at the story's end, and the sociality of the party is its contemptible counterpart. This supposed dualism in Joyce's story has been attenuated in postcolonial criticism at the turn of the century. Vincent Cheng, for example, had ridiculed in 1995 the pretensions of Gabriel and the party-goers for the dependence of their 'highly refined and "civilized" European culture of galoshes and pianos', on the 'gutta percha and ivory ripped out of colonial nations'. He had contrasted this civilized exploitation with 'the more primitive, unrestrained, and still uncolonized Irish free spirit allied symbolically

Plate 14.

to the West of Ireland'. However, by 2000, in the wake of reading Declan Kiberd and David Lloyd, Cheng came to define Ireland 'as a mongrel culture – even a culture of imposture, adulteration, and inauthenticity: modern and diverse in its variety and complexity – rather than primitive, premodern, and ineluctably Other by virtue of a narrowly defined, authentic otherness.'[67] These newly valorized terms now ascribe positive value to the culture of imposture and role-playing that may characterize the Misses Morkan's party and ascribe less value to what Cheng reveals to be Miss Ivors' playing of the 'authenticity-card'. The party appears now to be a benign *bricolage* of finding a way through with always inadequate resources, and the story's sublime ending to be a blow struck on behalf of an authenticity that millennial postcolonialism judges to be suspect.

It remains true, nevertheless, that 'criticism focuses on the ending'.[68] Huston's film, by contrast, focuses on the beginning and on the middle: on the party, its protocols, its small highlights, its disappointments, its impostures. Indeed, the film introduces a new instance of imposture and role-playing when it inserts an additional character, Mr Grace, who can so movingly mimic the poetic 'peasant' idiom of a young girl. In Huston's film the dinner and drawing-room scenes are made longer, and the hotel bedroom scene made shorter, relative to Joyce's story. As one reviewer of the film laconically noted:

> Far from being as lugubrious as the title might suggest, Huston's film . . . is a hymn to life. In the last 10 minutes, however, the remembrance of a young man's death brings a note of sadness to a Twelfth Night party.[69]

Such a response to the film serves to highlight and to call in question a literary critical consensus that had foregrounded 'the last 10 minutes' and seldom discovered in the party scene of Joyce's story 'a hymn to life'. The consensus that has valorized the ending of the story is certainly late Romantic in its assumptions: Shelleyan in its positive evaluation of unrequited love followed by an early death, and its negative evaluation of a polite urban social fabric of interdependency. The film puts this romantic consensus in doubt. We can see the effects of this doubt in Denis Donoghue's reading of Joyce's story immediately after seeing the film. Donoghue revises Kenneth Burke's reading of 'The Dead' as a story of superficial sociality followed by the revelation of a mystery. He now discovers a story that is more balanced in its structure. He severely modifies the charge of superficiality applied to the social formations represented in the story, and he allows a little less to the epiphanic ending:

> The form of Joyce's story is simple: from a web of domestic or social custom, a revelation arises. It need not be a great revelation, but it is enough to cause an 'epiphany', to rend the veil of a minor temple. In 'The Dead' the web is composed of the dance, the hospitality, the food and drink

. . . The dinner talk turns upon Dublin's musical and operatic life.

Donoghue's respect for custom (where others talk slightingly of mere decorum) disposes him to admire Huston's interpretation of the first long section of 'The Dead'. He judges the representation of Aunt Julia's singing to be a triumph of tact and appropriateness, and he admires Huston's film because 'No talk of moral paralysis has diverted Huston from acknowledging the merit of the sentiments, foibles, and passions he depicts. He never even considers making himself superior to them.'[70]

Huston, indeed, had always directed a sceptical eye towards romantic assumptions about the absolute value of first love and the unimportance of social superficialities. Huston's first film, *The Maltese Falcon* (1941), with its downbeat take on romance and on the lies implicit in romantic storytelling, can serve as the first instance. After a lifetime's work, Huston concluded: 'One is pressed to recall in which of my films the heroes failed, in which they succeeded. Their end doesn't mean much to me. It is the *company* in itself that constitutes an adventure.'[71] An exemplary instance, within Huston's *oeuvre*, of his respect for 'company' is *Fat City* (1972), with its undercutting of heroics, of the prize fighter and of young love. Lesley Brill, in his study of Huston's film-making, celebrates the patterning of the film by which the characters accommodate one another:

> Daily pleasures and irritants, small courtesies extended, assistance supplied – *Fat City* meditates on the common humanity expressed in ordinary people, gestures, and events. Billy Tully looks for a match to light the last cigarette of his pack as the story begins and will again be seeking a light just before it ends.[72]

The world of *Fat City*, set in Stockton, California, amidst the highways, rubble and hotels, is far removed in time and place from

Joyce's Dublin in 'The Dead'. Yet, in *The Dead* (as in much of Huston's *oeuvre*) we witness the dignity of social custom, politeness and strained courtesies, and the film gives more credit to those social customs than most critics of Joyce's story have been willing to do. Critics of Huston's film have implicitly recognized the new balance it strikes:

> Against divisive energies of nationality, city–country antagonisms, personal triangles, or class status are set the unifying influences of social ceremony and art. Most obvious is the dinner party itself, with its dances, its singing of 'for they are jolly good fellows', and other congenial rituals.[73]

The question then presents itself: how is it that Huston connects the party scene to the story's lonely ending? How does Huston overcome the problem, identified by Allen Tate, that 'no preparation, in its own terms, was possible' for the arrival of Michael Furey at the story's ending?[74] How does Huston avoid a film narrative that would fall short of the seamlessness expected of the classical Hollywood narrative?

One of the chief infidelities that Huston commits in order to connect the party scene to the story's denouement is the introduction of Mr Grace's recitation of 'Donal Óg'. The function of this insertion is to motivate and to determine the response of Gretta to the singing of 'The Lass of Aughrim' and to establish an associative connection between the middle and the end of the film. Mr Grace's recitation, one of the very few substantial additions made to Joyce's story by Huston's film, serves to place Gretta's final confession in a necessary sequence, begun with 'Donal Óg' (a translation of a Gaelic lament), repeated with 'The Lass of Aughrim', and realized finally in her own story of Michael Furey. She is set apart from the other young women at the party, without a doubt, but the film, by introducing into the drawing-room Mr Grace's recitation, must also discover a common ground of sympathy between all the 'ladies' who hear strange Western tales and songs of love.

In the drawing-room Mr Grace (Seán McClory) recites the dramatic monologue of a young girl who had been in love, and the editing of reaction shots lets the viewers of the film know that all the young women, and chiefly Gretta herself, fall under his spell. Gretta's response, a peculiar fixed angle of neck and head suddenly called to attention, as if woken out of a trance, becomes an attitude of the body that Anjelica Huston uses to define the discontinuity between Gretta's private and public character: her enigma in Gabriel's eyes. She enacts this identical gesture when Aunt Kate speaks about the tenor Parkinson, and also when Gabriel looks up at her on the staircase as she listens to Bartell D'Arcy's singing. In the film, but not in Joyce's story, Lily is present at the end of each of these moments of rapt attention. She acts as a counterpoint to a dreamy female gaze which she undercuts by her matter-of-factness.

> MR GRACE: You promised me a thing that is hard got you, a ship of gold under a silver mast: twelve towns and a market in all of them, and a fine white court by the side of the sea.
>
> *Mary Jane's Young Ladies.*
>
> *Clearly the author of the anonymous piece is a girl like themselves except that she is passionately in love.*
>
> MR GRACE: (cont'd.) You promised me a thing that is not possible; that you would give me gloves of the skin of a fish; that you would give me shoes of the skin of a bird and a suit of the dearest silk in Ireland. My mother said to me not to be talking with you, today or tomorrow or on Sunday. It was a bad time she took telling me that; it was shutting the door after the house was robbed.
>
> *Despite being a corpulent middle-aged academic, Mr Grace has somehow managed to transform himself utterly into the spirit of the speaker. Finally he looks directly into the faces of his listeners.*

MR GRACE: (cont'd.) You have taken the east from me, you have taken the west from me, you have taken what is before me and what is behind me; you have taken the moon, you have taken the sun from me, and my fear is great you have taken God from me.

His audience does not know how to react. There is an instance of complete silence.

MR GRACE: (cont'd.) It's from the Irish.

The Room.

As various voices rise in a chorus together.

AUNT KATE: *Very strange . . . but beautiful.*

MR BROWNE: I never heard anything like it.

MISS FURLONG: Very mysterious.

MISS HIGGINS: Can you imagine being in love like that?

MISS DALY: I thought it was beautiful.

BARTELL D'ARCY: It would make a lovely song.

Gabriel.

Clapping with the rest. He looks across at Gretta.

Gretta.

It is almost as if she were in a trance. Though her gaze is inward, an enigmatic beauty pours from her like that of a fine unsentimental picture of the Annunciation.

Gabriel.

Slightly baffled by the look on his wife's face. There is movement behind him. He looks round. It is Lily.[75]

The most striking ideological change that Huston's insertion of 'Donal Óg' effects is a generalizing of affective response to the Gaelic West. In Joyce's story, it is Gretta alone who is susceptible to the memory trace of the West, the trace of her own distinctive past, affections that set her apart from everyone else.

We might notice, for example, the contrast in Joyce's story between Gretta's and the Misses Morkan's response to the singing, 'in the old Irish tonality', of 'The Lass of Aughrim'. Mary Jane, in spite of being asked to hush by Gabriel, who points to his wife in raptures, interrupts and rushes towards the stairs, unmoved by the 'air' she hears:

> —It's Bartell D'Arcy singing, and he wouldn't sing all night.
>
> O, I'll get him to sing a song before he goes.
>
> —O, do, Mary Jane, said Aunt Kate.

In Huston's film, by contrast, Gretta shares her affective sense for a ballad and for a love story 'from the Irish': all the women, except Lily, now find these seductive. Perhaps none of the men do, with the exception of Mr Grace. Gretta remains distinctive, through the film's choreography of her response and through the steadily increasing centrality of her character on screen. Nevertheless, the balance of the original story is changed: at least as far as the 'young ladies' are concerned, the East now welcomes the West into the party scene, in a manner that simply does not happen in Joyce's story, except when Gabriel hears Gretta's story in the lonely hotel bedroom. In the film the affective encounter between East and West happens in both halves of the narrative, and binds them together.

The introduction of 'Donal Óg' has other effects also: it further complicates an already complicated set of analogies between male and female experience in Joyce's story. In particular, the insertion of Lily into the scene of the recitation and at its ending, with the continuous deep focus shot of her waiting silently for its conclusion, establishes a contrast in social class between her and the 'ladies' which cuts across identities of gender. It is not certain if the speaker of 'Donal Óg' is male or female, although the screenplay and common responses to the scene assume that the speaker is a young woman. Gretta's immersion in the recitation can be explained only by her hearing in its accusations the voice of Michael Furey. So, too, she must parallel the cold fate of 'The Lass of Aughrim' not with her own fate but with that of Michael

Furey. Both 'Donal Óg' and 'The Lass of Aughrim' are lyrics of complaint about abandonment in love. Too often critics have elided the discontinuity between victim and beloved when attaching one or both of these stories to Gretta's memories of Michael Furey. More than one critic claims that Gretta is nothing less than a latter-day 'Lass of Aughrim' (with Gabriel a tyrannical Lord Gregory safe and warm within his castle) and thereby it is alleged that Joyce's story is an allegory of the parallel power structures of patriarchal and colonial domination.[76]

However, the abandoned lover in Gretta's memories is not herself, but a young man whom she had left out in the cold. It was *she* who had remained protected within. Is she not more like the Lord Gregory of the song than Gabriel has any claim to be? Was Michael Furey, dying out in the wet cold, not more like the Lass? That association is strengthened in Huston's film because the words of the song are sung in full and echo in some detail the plight of Michael Furey outside Gretta's window on a night of remorseless rain. In 'Donal Óg' and in 'The Lass of Aughrim' the abandoned one can be assumed to be female. But this is not so in Gretta's memories of Michael Furey, whom she had left at the time when his health was 'much worse', and in spite of his desperate and fatal attempt to persuade her to stay. The gendering of suffering and loss and betrayal are not neatly aligned in Joyce's story or in Huston's film. Not the least of Gretta's emotions is guilt: the guilt of the beloved who refuses. In Huston's film, that complication, little noticed in a consensus of humanist and postcolonial criticism that has tended to idealize Gretta, is made all the more problematical by the insertion of an additional tale of love not returned. Mr Grace's recitation has a double narrative impact: both immediately within the drawing-room where it is told, and later within the hotel bedroom where it resonates.

It is possible to focus these complications in a brief analysis of *Another Woman* (1988) by Woody Allen. This film can be read as a loose version of 'The Dead', and is a version told, as it were, from Gretta's point of view. Written and directed by Woody Allen, and released a year after *The Dead*, *Another Woman* takes as its central character Marion Post (Gena Rowlands), a professor of philosophy at a New York women's college. She has just turned fifty and her marriage to Ken (Ian Holm) has begun to realize its inadequacies. Many years before, she had been passionately in love with a novelist, Larry Lewis (Gene Hackman), but had been unwilling to accept in herself the passionate desire she had felt for him. Moreover, a man has died for her: her first husband, Sam (Philip Bosco), had committed suicide some time after she had divorced him. The film is structured between party scenes and scenes of private time when one or sometimes two characters hold the screen. The drama of the film derives from a chance event: Marion overhears, through the ventilation grille in the room where she is writing, the voice of a young pregnant woman. This disembodied voice is that of Hope (Mia Farrow), and it betrays an extreme, perhaps suicidal, grief of which Hope is speaking to an analyst in the apartment below. Hope's grieving voice, like the singing of 'The Lass of Aughrim' in both Huston's film and Joyce's story, catapults the protagonist's mind into her own past, into her memories of loss and of guilt about an opportunity for love that had once been offered to her.

Unlike the narratives of Joyce and of Huston, *Another Woman* both sympathizes with and offers a critique of the female character at its centre. She is the narrative focus of a story that is told from her own point of view; she is the victim of a lost love, but the responsibility for its loss is also hers: she refused love for reasons she judged to be in her own interest. Indeed, Rossellini's *Voyage to Italy* submits Katherine (Ingrid Bergman) to a gaze that is equally compassionate and sceptical. However, no such ambiguity is attached to Gretta Conroy within almost all critical interpretations of Joyce's story: her idealization is a common assumption but, once called into focus by its overdetermination in Huston's film, it becomes questionable. That question is best analysed by Margot Norris, who re-assesses the function in Joyce's story of 'The Aestheticized Gretta'. She urges readers of the story to give a more sceptical attention both to the narrator's complicity in idealizing Gretta and to the story's feminist devices that undermine what she judges to be the story's suffocating narrator. Those devices include the story's implicit celebration of female back answers and silences, by Lily, Molly Ivors, Aunt Kate and Gretta herself. Norris proposes that readers align themselves with Miss Ivors running down the stairs to escape, in preference to Gretta standing on the stairs so picturesquely.[77]

Joyce himself raised a question about Gretta's status in his own later rewriting of 'The Dead' for another medium. His play *Exiles* (1913) can be described as a version of 'The Dead' for the theatre. In his notes on *Exiles* Joyce discusses the relationship of the play's protagonists, Bertha and Richard, and he revisits the same moment in Nora Barnacle's past that informs both *Exiles* and 'The Dead': her childhood relationship with a youth in Galway. Joyce identifies in his notes the romantic assumptions about young fatal love, and the gothic world of ghosts and of corpses, when he compares the burial of the blond Shelley in Rome with that of the dark Sonny Bodkin (Michael Furey) in Rahoon.

> She sees his tomb . . . and weeps. . . . In the convent they called her the man-killer . . . Rome is the strange world and strange life to which Richard brings her. Rahoon her people. She weeps over Rahoon too, over him whom her love has killed, the dark boy . . . He is her buried life, her past. . . . There are tears of commiseration. She is Magdalen who weeps remembering the loves she could not return.[78]

Huston's introduction of the recitation of 'Donal Óg' by Mr Grace, with its narrative of love not returned and of broken vows, overcomes a structural problem in 'The Dead'. It is the problem defined by Allen Tate, that 'no preparation, in its own terms, was possible' for the arrival of Michael Furey at the story's ending. It is the same problem as that first identified by the anonymous reviewer in the *Times Literary Supplement* on the story's first publication: 'The issue seems trivial, and the connecting thread becomes so tenuous as to be scarcely perceptible.'[79]

While effecting that structural continuity, Mr Grace's recitation introduces fascinating new imbalances between gender, class and audience. The 'young ladies' and Gretta are moved by the recitation; Lily, who knows something different about love's promises, is not. Lily's appearance on the screen in deep focus and her blunt statement about the food dislocate the audience of the film from the audience of the recitation. The accentuation of Lily's screen presence at this moment alerts the audience of the film to a new possibility that remains unrecognized by the ladies and gentlemen in the drawing-room: an alignment of a social underclass against those who aestheticize loss. That alignment places Lily the caretaker's daughter with Michael Furey the employee in a gasworks, with the Lass of Aughrim a homeless outcast, with the illegal alien and maid, Maricela, to whom the film is dedicated. That alignment places Gretta Conroy, in spite of the camera's aestheticization of her pose on the stairs, with those who refuse, and who suffer, the luxury of nostalgia.

7

IN THE HOTEL BEDROOM: THE JAMES JOYCE
CRITICAL INDUSTRY

If Mr Grace's recitation in the drawing-room is a flagrant addition to Joyce's story, Huston's film makes its most subtle deletion from the story during the final scene in the hotel bedroom. The deletion is subtle because it is the erasure of a blank space in the text: the double-line space between the sentence that tells us that Gabriel walked quietly to the window and the sentence that tells us that Gretta was fast asleep. What happens in that blank space on the page? What time has passed? How have the protagonists rearranged themselves? How have the objects in the room been redistributed? The answers provided by the text are both definite and suggestive. The double-line space has seldom troubled readers, but its deletion by the film allows us now to focus upon its importance and to wonder that critics, no less than Huston's film, have passed over it in silence.

Before the double-line space, Gretta is awake and crying, fully clothed, lying on the quilt, and Gabriel stands fully clothed by the window. After the double-line space, Gabriel is naked in bed, Gretta lies under the covers, her mouth half-open, her clothes thrown over a chair: 'A petticoat string dangled to the floor. One boot stood upright, its limp upper fallen down: the fellow of it lay upon its side.' Gabriel also lies upon his side, leaning on his elbow, turned towards his wife. He settles further under the sheets because the room is chilly. After the taps on the window, he turns over and looks towards it and towards the snow that has started to fall again.

By excising the gap on the page, the film excises also all the events that have occurred (and may have occurred) in that explicit lacuna in the story: the undressing of Gabriel and of Gretta, their lying in bed together, perhaps their intercourse, after which she sleeps and he reflects on what he has (and has not) been told: 'Perhaps she had not told him all the story. His eyes moved to the chair over which she had thrown some of her clothes.' The film provides for no intervening events. Therefore, in the film Gabriel speaks his final words from a distinctly different point of view than in the story: standing at the window in lonely transcendence instead of lying in bed in what may be a reverie, or a post-coital blur.

Let us look at the screenplay and at the film. After Gretta's exclamation 'O, the day I heard that, that he was dead!' the screenplay and the film at first obey exactly the sentences of the text. The screenplay's only emendation is of the past to the present tense, as in the instructions to the actors:

> *Choking with sobs and overcome by emotion, Gretta flings herself downward on the bed, sobbing into the quilt. Gabriel holds her hand for a moment longer, irresolutely, and then, shy of*

Plate 15.

intruding on her grief, lets it fall gently and walks quietly to the
window.

It is here that the double-line space occurs in Joyce's text. The
screenplay deletes this silent pause and the lapse of time that it
represents. A wipe or a fade might have been used in the film as
equivalent to the text's white space. After the wipe or fade, the new
configuration of persons and things could have been presented to
viewers of the film. Nothing of the kind happens. Instead, the action
immediately continues with the commencement of a monologue,
composed of sentences selected from the text's last five paragraphs,
delivered as a voice-over by Gabriel as he arrives to stand at the
window:

Exterior Window from Gabriel's P.O.V.
As snow starts falling again.
Close on Gabriel.
As he looks out at the window at the falling snow.
Close on Gretta.
Fast asleep, her hair tangled, her mouth half open.
  GABRIEL: [off-screen] So you had that romance in your life?
  – a man died for your sake.
Gabriel.
  GABRIEL: (cont'd.) Strange it hardly pains me now to think
  how poor a part I've played in your life. It's almost as though
  I'm not your husband, that we've never lived together as
  man and wife. What were you like then, in the time of your
  first girlish beauty?
Close on marks of age on Gretta's face.
  GABRIEL: [off-screen] (cont'd.) To me your face is still
  beautiful . . . but it is no longer the one for which Michael
  Furey braved death.
Close on Gabriel.

GABRIEL: V.O. (cont'd) Why am I feeling this riot of emotion? What stirred it up? The ride in the cab? – her not responding when I kissed her hand? . . . my aunt's party? . . . my own foolish speech? . . . wine? . . . dancing? . . . music? Poor Aunt Julia! . . . that haggard look on her face when she was singing 'Arrayed for the Bridal' . . . Soon she'll be a shade too with the shade of Patrick Morkan and his horse.

Insert of a distant hill with a lonely churchyard at the top.

GABRIEL: V.O. (cont'd.) Better to pass boldly into that other world, in the full glory of some passion, than fade and wither dismally with age!

Close on Gabriel seen through the falling snow standing at the window.

GABRIEL: V.O. (cont'd.) How long had you locked in your heart the image of your lover's eyes when he told you he did not wish to live! I've never felt that way myself towards any woman but I know that such a feeling must be love.

Insert of a graveyard with snow falling.

GABRIEL: V.O. (cont'd.) Think of all those who ever were . . . back to the start of time . . . and me, transient as they . . . flickering out as well into their grey world . . . like everything around me . . . this solid world itself which they reared and lived in is dwindling and dissolving.

Inserts of ancient monuments with snow falling.

GABRIEL: V.O. (cont'd.) Snow is falling . . . falling in that lonely churchyard where Michael Furey lies buried . . .

Insert of snow falling on barren thorns.

GABRIEL: V.O. (cont'd.) . . . falling faintly through the universe and faintly falling, like the descent of their last end, upon the living and the dead.

Camera pans up to the night sky until flakes of snow fall directly into the lens.

Fade Out.
The End.[80]

There are several contrasts that can be made here between the screenplay and the film as it exists on screen. In the film, but not in the screenplay, Gabriel briefly passes the mirror on his way to the window. We do not see on screen the many close-ups of Gretta and Gabriel that the screenplay proposes. In the film Gretta's mouth is not 'half open' as the screenplay, copying from the story, declares. The inserts are more specific on screen than the screenplay suggests: inserts of bogs, ruins, Celtic crosses, a round tower, thorns, sky and snow. These differences between screenplay and film are slight enough. There are also slight differences between film and story: between, for example, the selected phrases and their exact occurrence in Joyce's text. The film's 'To me your face is still beautiful' is more benign than the narrator's double negative, 'He did not like to say even to himself that her face was no longer beautiful.' The film's 'Why am I feeling this riot of emotion?' betrays its compacting of the slower and more changeable narrative time of Joyce's story, as reflected in 'He wondered at his riot of emotions of an hour before'. In the film, only minutes have passed. Similarly, the deletion of Gabriel's decision that 'The time had come for him to set out on his journey westward' appears remarkable, but many have thought it is compensated for by the film's other method of compacting meaning: the montage of ruins, graveyards, Celtic crosses and a round tower.

I wish to focus in the first instance on the ways in which the bedroom scene in the film appears consistent with the story, while its deletions change the story's very structure, in particular its definition of point of view. Whereas Joyce's story represents a Gabriel who is unstable in his affections, inner divisions, reversals of mood and desire, Huston's film delivers a Gabriel who, though deeply moving, is integrated in a single continuity of compassion. That continuity is defined on screen both in his bodily responses to Gretta's story and in his final internal monologue. Huston's film, that is to say, shares the expectations that are celebrated in canonical literary criticism that Gabriel, at the story's end, is a sexless transcendent idealist.[81]

Let us be specific about this critical agreement. For Allen Tate in 1950, Gabriel escapes 'from his own ego into the larger world of humanity, including "all the living and the dead"'. For Kenneth Burke in 1954, 'Gabriel can at last arrive at the order of ideal sociality . . . the world of conditions as seen through the spirit of conditions transcended, of ideal sociality beyond material divisiveness.' For C. C. Loomis Jr. in 1960, 'We move from the general to the particular, then to a final universal. We see Gabriel's world . . . we are given a universal symbol in the vision itself'. For Florence L. Walzl in 1966, 'Gabriel's swoon is a symbolic death from which he will rise revivified. Gabriel is rightly named: he is a figure of annunciation and new life.'[82] This consensus is strong enough to include even those who claim to challenge it. Vincent Cheng, in *Joyce, Race, and Empire* (1995), does little more than add one further character to Gabriel's already inclusive list of humanity by twisting the word 'shade' from its reference to ghosts and directing its reference to skin pigmentation. Cheng concludes:

> Gabriel's final vision of the falling snow which 'was general all over Ireland' attempts to break down the barriers of difference constructed by the patriarchal ego he is so deeply (if unconsciously) implicated in, into at least a recognition of generosity and sameness, all shades of equal color, whether these 'shades . . . pass[ing] boldly into that other world' be Michael Furey, Aunt Julia, black opera singers, or himself.[83]

Indeed Cheng, who imagines his reading of the story to be troubling for older scholars because it is overtly political, reverts here to the phrasing first used by Allen Tate: 'a shared or a collective subjectivity, allowing the ego to dissolve'. Historically, it is Richard Ellmann who gives this agreement its strongest authority, and it was perhaps Ellmann himself who may inadvertently have lent authority to Huston's positioning of Gabriel at the window in the final scene of the film. For Ellmann implies a strong misreading of Joyce when he describes how the vision of the final mutual symbolic snow is 'seen from the window of the hotel'.[84]

It seems to me a useful exercise, therefore, to imagine an alternative final scene for Huston's film, a scene that accords more closely with Joyce's own directions: a scene in which (after a fade or wipe) the camera focuses on Gabriel, who, as Joyce's story directs, lies naked in bed. The camera then surveys the dishevelled bedroom, the underclothes, the boots. Turning his upper body away from Gretta to face the window, again as Joyce's story directs, Gabriel watches 'sleepily' the flakes of snow against the lamplight. The status of Gabriel's words, beginning with his doubts about his wife's truth-telling, would be altered by such cinematic fidelity to Joyce's story. The bedroom scene would be altered from its conformity with the idealizing interpretations of Ellmann and others. Gabriel's words would not so easily evoke the favoured terms of a universal and ideal vision of humanity, if spoken from such a doubtful point of view. Indeed, the sleepiness of his gaze might evoke instead suggestions of lullaby or sing-song and the rhythms of his words – 'falling softly', 'softly falling', 'falling faintly', 'faintly falling' – might seem to lull him to sleep rather than awake him to metaphysical truths.

John Paul Riquelme has drawn our attention to the echolalia and rhythmic repetition of sounds in the final sentence of Joyce's story:

> The sentence's echoic language includes, for example, a great deal of sibilance ('*s*oul *s*wooned *s*lowly . . . *s*now . . . univer*s*e . . . de*s*cent'), numerous repetitions of liquid consonants ('sou*l* . . . s*l*owly . . . fa*ll*ing faint*l*y . . . faint*l*y

falling, like . . . last . . . all . . . living'), examples of assonance ('soul . . . slowly . . . snow'), and an instance of chiasmus ('falling faintly . . . faintly falling'). Any sentence that possesses this kind of phonetically echoic character, which we expect in lyric poetry but not in realistic stories, enables a reader to generate meanings that may not be evident or that may not be emphasized semantically.[85]

Riquelme's account of dense phonetic repetitions is valuable, and can alert us to the possibility that Gabriel's last words mimic other processes than the generation of symbolic meanings. Such echoic patterns of repetition and inversion function not so much in lyric poetry in general as in that particular subset of lyric, the lullaby, with its slow repetitive patterns: 'Hushaby baby on the tree top, When the wind blows the cradle will rock, When the bough breaks, the cradle will fall, And down will come baby, cradle and all.' Here the excess of echoic repetition overwhelms and subdues any stable meaning whatsoever. Echolalia is an index of a lapsing into unconsciousness, not a summoning of words into conscious order. Joyce's story and Huston's film are not equal at the end in their use of echoic patterns. The story, with its greater number of echoic patterns, allows more for the possibility of a beneath-the-sheets sleepy blur than does the film. The film includes less echolalia in its selection from Gabriel's last words, and allows no recumbent final posture to the protagonist.

The use of a voice-over monologue to give stable form to the unstable concluding words of Joyce's text should provoke our anxiety. It was an anxious move by the film-makers themselves. The choice of Gabriel's voice was not the first option they tried. The first experiment was an ending in which there was no voice, no words, only music and a montage of images. The second was a third-person narrator, reciting the final paragraphs, in a voice that is not Gabriel's. Finally, the choice was made to combine montage, music and

Gabriel's own voice spoken, as it were, to himself.[86] For critics of film and story, the question about the status of the extraordinary last three paragraphs of Joyce's text has been put most vividly in the form: 'Who speaks these lines?' James Naremore offers the best response: 'We can't give a completely satisfactory answer to the question, and that is the whole point.'[87]

Perhaps it is for this reason that critics have been able to read the story's ending in such contrary ways. Indeed, as Elizabeth Butler Cullingford has noticed:

> The end of 'The Dead' is a political Rorschach blot for Joyceans. Joep Leerssen agrees with John Wilson Foster that the journey westward is deathly, Michael Furey another Count Dracula, and the past a nightmare from which no one can escape . . . But Seamus Deane endorses the views of [Vincent] Cheng, [Luke] Gibbons, [and Emer] Nolan . . . when he claims that 'an actual space for liberation open[s], in the west of Miss Ivors and Michael Furey.'[88]

The unstable narrative structure of Joyce's story and the conflict of interpretations it has provoked depend upon the instability of the narrative voice. This Joycean device is first defined by Hugh Kenner in *Joyce's Voices* (1978). His initial example is the opening sentence of 'The Dead': 'Lily, the caretaker's daughter, was literally run off her feet.' A covert, reliable, third-person narrative voice would have been more exact. The sentence would have read: 'Lily, the caretaker's daughter, was (figuratively) run off her feet.' Joyce's method, Kenner explains, makes narration look like objective report, but in fact the narration is tinged with the idiom of the person described. A free indirect discourse of this kind provokes specific uncertainties about who is responsible for reported thoughts or speech. 'It was always a great affair, the Misses Morkan's annual dance.' Who speaks these words? Are they to be attributed to some unnamed character or are they the suffocating and smug assurances of a reliable narrator? Reliable third-person and unreliable first-person narratives merge in a volatile element that is always challenging for the reader to test and to trust. Joyce's fictions, Kenner tells us, 'tend not to have a detached narrator, though they seem to have . . . One reason the quiet little stories of *Dubliners* continue to fascinate is that the narrative point of view unobtrusively fluctuates . . . one person's sense of things inconspicuously giving place to another's.' Readers of 'The Dead' are told in the first paragraph that the party guests are 'ladies' and 'gentlemen', but, when readers notice that these are Lily's terms, the status of the guests becomes relatively uncertain and remains so.[89] Indeed, readers have variously described the party as attended by the petit bourgeoisie, the lower middle class, the middle class, and even the upper middle class of Dublin. Such uncertainty proceeds from a textually unfixed point of view, whether it be that of a narrator or of a character of whatever social class, say Lily's or Mary Jane's: all categories show relative slippage.

Film and narrative fiction are often thought to be alike in their management of point of view, character and event. The eye of the camera is sometimes compared to the omniscient eye of a third-person narrator in prose fiction, surveying the world of things and persons and placing them in a dynamic order.[90] However, the worlds of verbal and of visual signifiers can evoke quite different responses in reader or viewer. Furthermore, the camera eye has no direct access to a world of thought or feeling, which the omniscient narrative voice lays claim to as it freely moves in and out of characters' hearts and minds: 'The camera is not omniscient like the nineteenth-century narrator nor is its powerful intimacy as subjective as a stream-of-consciousness narrative.'[91] If the camera can replicate neither third-person nor first-person narrative voices, it most certainly cannot replicate the uncertain and volatile merging of both voices that Kenner describes. This is perhaps the most awkward structural difference between Joyce's 'The Dead' and Huston's film version. The distinctive style of Joyce's story is its scrupulous use of undetermined points of view. Even the most sympathetic critics of the film admit, however, that 'The oscillating point of view in Joyce's narrative proves to be impossible to achieve in film.'[92]

This incommensurable difference between story and film is most evident in the final three paragraphs, which take their bearings from Gabriel's state of mind. Readers of the text of Joyce's story must shift as best they can, from phrase to phrase, in order to decide the status and authority of a volatile narrative voice (third-person, first-person, or both at once):

> It had begun to snow again. He watched sleepily the flakes, silver and dark, falling obliquely against the lamplight. The time had come for him to set out on his journey westward. Yes, the newspapers were right: snow was general all over Ireland. It was falling on every part of the dark central plain.

In these sentences we can discover, rapidly, third-person and first-person narrative voices, and a free indirect discourse that merges and separates both in uncertain ways. For example, it remains uncertain if the narrator, or Gabriel, or both, have decided that a journey westward is required. It remains uncertain, also, if the words about snow being general all over Ireland are a deeply felt reflection or merely a parodic quotation from Mary Jane's chatter about the weather forecast when the guests were leaving the party. Translated to the screen, in the closing moments of Huston's film, all questions of voice, all questions about who speaks, all doubts about parody, are removed. The voice is Gabriel's. His lips do not move, but it is recognizably his voice, and the articulation of his (and only his) transparent thought and feeling. The film's music and the inserted montage of landscape images expand, define and confirm the stability of Gabriel's mood, its guaranteed subjectivity, and its world of reference.[93]

Nevertheless, the insertion of a montage of images of gravestones, water, a round tower, fields, all covered by snow, has provoked some differences of interpretation of the film, not unlike those occasioned by the Rorschach blot of Joyce's text. For Clive Hart these images (like 'shots shown to neighbours on return from a winter holiday') weaken the film's ending, although they do not quite ruin its true sense of 'the growth of love through a transcendence of the self'.[94] For Lesley Brill, these last images of Huston's directorial art stand as an index of Huston's work, his sense of limit and of death: 'the sea; the sky; and flecks of light against a darkness that will finally assume dominion, both at the end of the film and at the end of life'.[95] For John Simon, who disapproves of all adaptations of literary art to the screen, 'It looks like a travelogue, the lowliest of cinematic genres, and no match for deathless prose'.[96] For other critics more preoccupied with Irish cultural politics, the montage and the voice-over combine to nudge Joyce's text beyond its alleged reticence into an overtly political statement of nationalist liberation:

> The words in their original form summon up memories of private grief but in the film the flight westward is given a wider political interpretation. Images of a lonely graveyard, shrouded in snow, are linked to the silhouetted remains of round towers and monastic ruins, emblems of a golden age in nationalist history. Headstones may signify death but monuments in nationalist iconography are signs of a new beginning, harbingers of a political and cultural awakening. Gabriel's earlier refusal, as an urban cosmopolite, to accompany the nationalist Miss Ivors on a visit to the west of Ireland, means that he is cut off not only from the enigma of his wife's inner life, but also from his own repressed cultural identity. In Huston's version we are allowed a

glimpse of Joyce's political as well as his personal unconscious.[97]

It is clear from these very different readings that any viewer of the film may comply with Huston's description of how film 'throws onto the screen that which [the viewer] *wants* to see'. This subjective effect is most vividly highlighted in the filming of the montage sequence of gravestones, bushes and heritage monuments by the film's Second Unit, based in Ireland under Irish locations manager Seamus Byrne. This Second Unit had responsibility for external shots, not only those of the carriage travelling along the Liffey quays or of the exterior of the house on Usher's Island, but also of the landscape montage at the film's ending. The locations for the montage may appear to viewers of the film as iconic signs of the West, but they are no such thing. Instead, the shots are of the eastern and midland counties: of County Kildare, in particular a graveyard near the Curragh; of County Wicklow, in particular the round tower at Glendalough; and of the Rock of Cashel in County Tipperary. These 'bits of Irish Irishness', according to Seamus Byrne, were selected in these specific locations 'because there was natural snow lying there'.[98]

For Molly Ivors, the West is Aran and Connacht; for Gretta, the West is the city of Galway; for Gabriel, it is an embarrassment. Marjorie Howes has shown that in Joyce's work the metaphorical geography of nationalism or unionism is subject to slippages of scale, locality and region. Such slippage can be seen in the different meanings of the West for Molly Ivors, Gretta and Gabriel. Slippage too can be seen when we notice that the midlands are indeed west of Dublin. They are, of course, not 'western' in the symbolic framework attributed to 'The Dead', but they are 'western' in the material sense that a 'lazy Dubliner' must cross the 'uninspiring' midlands to approach the symbolic nationalist West. This necessary dull journey is recognized in the last paragraph of the story and also in the voice-over of the film, both of which list the dark central plain, the treeless hills, the Bog of Allen.[99] There is, however, an overdetermination of that middle landscape in John Huston's film and it derives from the contingency required by the very process of editing montage. Montage in film is always subject to processes of fabrication and opportunism, and these were availed of by Seamus Byrne's Second Unit when selecting the sites for insertion. The film, therefore, concedes a material recognition of the symbolically empty space between East and West. For it is from that symbolically empty space that the montage images of 'Irish Irishness' are taken: by accident, because of a local fall of snow; by necessity, because the complexities of historical geography exceed the nationalist iconography of East, West and excluded middle.

8

IN THE MISSES MORKAN'S BATHROOM: JOHN HUSTON'S *OEUVRE*

Int. bathroom

Gabriel splashes cold water on Freddy Malins' face and tidies him up.

GABRIEL: Now you'll pass muster.

FREDDY: Then, if you'll excuse me, I've never been able to relieve myself in the presence of another, otherwise I'd have joined the army. Even as a child . . .

GABRIEL: Yes, yes, I understand.

FREDDY: The same was true of my father before me. When he went racing he'd wait, 'til the horses were running, to go to the lavatory. Anything under a mile and he'd miss the finish.[100]

Huston here avails of the opportunism that collaborative work can provide. The opportunity arose on the set of the film when Donal McCann had made the crew laugh with anecdotes about his father, including this anecdote about his father's inability to relieve himself except in absolute privacy.[101] Huston made use of McCann's story not least to illustrate Freddy Malins' fragile personality and Gabriel's correspondent sense of responsibility (Plate 16). But the episode does much more. It alerts viewers of the film to the way in which *The Dead* exemplifies a thematic preoccupation that recurs throughout Huston's movies: the representation of male failure and its incapacity to express itself. Both the detractors and the admirers of Huston's work acknowledge that the representation of male failure, failure that drains his protagonists' potency for action, remains its common thread. *The Dead* is one further articulation of this theme, a theme that sets Huston apart from other definitive *auteurs* of North American action cinema.

Plate 16.

The *locus classicus* for detraction of the work of John Huston is Andrew Sarris' judgement in *The American Cinema: Directors and Directions, 1927–1968*. Sarris asserts that Huston's

> theme has been remarkably consistent from *The Maltese Falcon* to *Reflections in a Golden Eye*. His protagonists almost invariably fail at what they set out to do, generally through no fault or flaw of their own. Unfortunately, Huston is less a pessimist than a defeatist, and his characters manage to be unlucky without the world being particularly out of joint . . . Unfortunately, Huston, unlike [Howard] Hawks, does not believe sufficiently in the action ethos to enjoy action for its own sake.[102]

An admirer of Huston, Pauline Kael, defined her respect for his work and her contempt for *auteurist* critics such as Sarris when she noted that they had championed Howard Hawks with all his 'sex and glamour and fantasies of the high-school boys' universe'.[103] Huston's representations of male failure had already received praise outside the United States. 'In France', Huston had noted in 1958, 'I learned last month or so that they've got me all figured out as an existentialist who preaches a philosophy of failure. I admit there's a lot of that in my films whether you go back to *The Maltese Falcon* or *The Red Badge of Courage* or the later ones.'[104]

The representation of male failure in Huston's *oeuvre* can be vividly summarized by bringing to mind Curtin (Tim Holt) and Dobbs (Humphrey Bogart) in *The Treasure of the Sierra Madre* (1948), Dix Handley (Sterling Hayden) in *The Asphalt Jungle* (1950), 'The Youth' (Audie Murphy) in *The Red Badge of Courage* (1951), Gay Langland (Clark Gable) in *The Misfits* (1961), and Billy Tully (Stacy Keach) and Ernie Munger (Jeff Bridges) in *Fat City* (1972). In *The Dead*, Freddy Malins' embarrassment about passing urine evokes once more the reticence of innumerable failed men in Huston's movies. In particular, it evokes the conversation between the men in *Fat City* about their memories of passing blood in their urine, and their anxieties about not making their women feel sexually fulfilled. It evokes a moment on screen in that film when the damaged prize fighter, Billy Tully's opponent, watches the blood from his haemorrhaging kidneys spill out into the toilet in his urine. At that moment we, the viewers, share his point of view. Professionally and sexually, men's bodies let them down, and their only rescue in Huston's movies is the camera's patient gaze.

Freddy Malins is no prize fighter, and his talk about joining the army will not enlist him among failed heroes, but his embarrassment about his phallus and about relieving himself in public places him among Huston's failed men, the aheroic ones. Freddy's embarrassment in the bathroom serves, in the structure of *The Dead*, as a proleptic instance not only of the final humiliation of the film's protagonist, Gabriel, but also that of Mr Browne, who gradually loses

Plate 17.

the bodily composure of his arrival at the party (Plate 7) and collapses into the physical befuddlement and frustration of his departure. No women in the film suffer this common male humiliation.

The particular ambiguity of Huston's representation of men and of the male body depends upon indices of sexual impotence or inertia, of fear and cowardice, of traditional heroic intentions drained, or defeated, or confused. Ineptitude and the refusal of sexual desire that is freely offered (Dix Handley), the collapse of public and family respect in a saloon bar (Gay Langland), the inert loneliness and shared silence at the counter of a diner (Billie Tully and Ernie Munger), all require some fragile consolation that company or, in the final instance, only the camera can offer. Gaylin Studlar confronts this ambiguity of such male failure in a male world when she defines the fundamental question raised by Huston's work as 'the relationship between fascination with masculine failure and the kinds of pleasure that film spectators might derive from Huston's films'.[105]

Plate 18.

In *The Dead*, the spectator's pleasure may derive from the camera's management of the transformation of Gabriel's body from that of a figure of control (Plates 6, 16), to a figure of anxious wonder (Plate 17), to a figure of lonely defeat. In terms of mirrors and the stability of the self, it is a complex movement. Gabriel can distance himself via Freddy from his own mirror image in the bathroom (Plate 16), and can stabilize the gaze of all companions at the dinner table (Plate 2). Yet he is, from time to time, an anxious figure (Plate 18). It is this anxious Gabriel who observes Gretta's averted gaze in the glass of the carriage and is humiliated in the hotel bedroom as he moves away from Gretta and briefly passes his own mirror image. In the final shot of Gabriel we, the film's audience, contemplate his face through the window as if he were gazing into an empty mirror. We at this final moment are privileged to observe Gabriel's defeat from that impossible point of view, the mirror's dark side. That privileged point of view permits the film's audience to become what Freddy Malins most feared: spectators to a man's privacy.

Preoccupation with self-conscious male failure allows *The Dead* to be seen less as a specifically Irish film than as part of a tradition of North American anti-Hollywood movies. Martin Rubin has observed that 'Hollywood cinema is a fundamentally heroic cinema because of its allegiance to classical narrative forms and its economic dependence on the star system.' He demonstrates how Huston worked to oppose Hollywood male heroics in *The Treasure of the Sierra Madre* (1948) and *The Red Badge of Courage* (1951):

> Huston's films frequently involve a destabilization of the hero position. This can take two basic forms: to prevent, delay, or otherwise impede the establishment of a hero position; and to undercut or devalue a hero position that has apparently been established. These tactics create abnormal difficulties and strain in the maintenance of a hero position, although they do not necessarily negate it altogether.[106]

The Dead opts for the second form described here: the undercutting or devaluation of a hero position established by Gabriel. We can notice, for example, that the film adds a brief episode as the guests depart when Gabriel must briefly submit to the higher professional status of Mr Grace and must reassure him that exam marks will be submitted on time. The overall effect achieved by the film is the devaluation of the status of Gabriel as protagonist. To address this process in *The Dead* is to propose not only a North American anti-Hollywood Huston, but a French Huston: a Huston whose first directorial success was not in cinema at all but in the theatre when he directed the première of Jean-Paul Sartre's *Huis Clos/No Exit* in New York in 1946. In that play two women and one man are enclosed in the hell they make for one another, an inverted version of the triangle that underlies Joyce's 'The Dead'. Later, Huston would secure Sartre's collaboration in order to make the film *Freud: The Secret Passion* in 1962.[107] In between those two productions, in the mid-1950s, Huston resolved to film Joyce's story of Gabriel Conroy's existential and sexual failure.

In *The Dead*, therefore, the episode of textual infidelity in the Misses Morkan's bathroom invites us to see the film not as a distinctively Irish film, but as an anti-Hollywood American movie, even as a French movie, which happens to be set in Ireland. Yet it is a version of 'The Dead' peculiarly consistent with one of the first reviews of Joyce's stories on their appearance in 1914:

> It is in so far as they are failures that his characters interest Mr Joyce. One of them – a capable washerwoman – falls an easy prey to a rogue in a tramcar and is cozened out of the little present she was taking to her family. Another – a trusted cashier – has so ordered a blameless life that he drives to drink and suicide the only person in the world with whom he was in sympathy. A third – an amiable man of letters –

learns at the moment he feels most drawn to his wife that her heart was given once and for all to a boy long dead.[108]

The Dead is a film about failure and displays those features of inertia that Andrew Sarris had regretted in Huston's work. Indeed, the milieu of *The Dead* is what Sarris wrongly thought Huston most disliked: 'that sissy stuff in drawing-rooms where people try to communicate with each other through dialogue'.[109] The representation of inertia was something that had troubled many who worked with Huston. When he accepted Arthur Miller's script for *The Misfits*, Huston left Miller with the task of persuading Clark Gable to accept the part of Gay Langland. Gable was resistant and it was difficult to persuade him that a western bereft of male heroism could work. Miller reported that Gable did not 'understand how you could do a picture that was in western costume and in a western setting where the audience would expect certain things to happen, and they weren't gonna happen. He was going by the old signposts.' Finally, using the symbolic geography of the United States, Miller told Gable: 'It's sort of an Eastern western. It's about our lives' meaninglessness and maybe how we got to where we are.'[110]

It is a giant step from the backcountry of Nevada and the codes of anti-heroes in *The Misfits* to the polite, if troubled, drawing-room of Edwardian Dublin in *The Dead*. Yet, for all that, *The Dead* maintains Huston's New World preoccupation with masculine failure in an Old World milieu. In its own idiom, the story of Gabriel and Michael in *The Dead* can be read, like that of other Huston films, as 'sort of an Eastern western'.

9

BEFORE 'THE DEAD': AFTER *THE DEAD*

The primary context for reading Joyce's story 'The Dead' is to sit with a copy of *Dubliners* in your hand. The context for viewing Huston's film *The Dead* is the darkness of a cinema or a night at home with the video. Viewed as an independent story, taken out of the context of *Dubliners*, 'The Dead' is likely to be interpreted in quite a different way to when read as the conclusion to a highly structured collection. The film greatly accentuates the story's autonomy as a stand-alone narrative, or a novella, as it is described on the title page of the film's screenplay. Indeed, at its world première in Venice, the film erased all the other stories in the collection and took to itself the title *Gente di Dublino*.

Even before the film was made, it had become clear that readers were divided between those who read the story in the context of the structured series of stories that Joyce called his 'moral history', and those who analysed it as a stand-alone narrative. As early as 1966 Florence Walzl identified two different kinds of readers of 'The Dead': those who interpret the story as the conclusion to what has gone before in *Dubliners*, and those who read the story by itself:

> For the reader who has come to this conclusion by way of the fourteen preceding stories of disillusioned children, frustrated youths, sterile adults and paralyzed social groups in *Dubliners*, the cosmic vision of 'The Dead' seems the last stage in a moribund process. The final fate of the *Dubliners* everyman is a death in life, and Gabriel Conroy's illumination is that he is dead. In this interpretation the vision is a final statement of the death themes of the book.

The snow that covers all Ireland images the deadly inertia of the nation. The lonely churchyard where Michael Furey lies buried pictures the end of individual hope and love. The crooked crosses on which the snow drifts represent the defective and spiritually dead Irish Church. The spears and barren thorns suggest the futility of Christ's sacrifice for a people so insensible. To the hero it is an irrevocable last judgment. Such an intepretation is a powerful and symbolically logical conclusion to *Dubliners*.

This is not the conclusion that the reader who knows only 'The Dead' draws. Interpreting the journey westward as a start toward a new life of greater reality, he sees a succession of rebirth images. The snow, though it is general over Ireland, is quickly swallowed in the Shannon waves . . . The judgment that Michael brings is a salvation, and Gabriel's swoon is a symbolic death from which he will rise revivified. Gabriel is rightly named: he is a figure of annunciation and new life.[111]

In February 1906 Grant Richards had accepted for publication a collection of fourteen stories beginning with 'The Sisters' and ending with 'Grace'. He thought better of his decision and rejected the volume that September. We owe 'The Dead', at least in some part, to Grant Richards' change of mind. Joyce completed 'The Dead' in September 1907, a year after Richards' rejection. The adding of 'The Dead' to the 1906 version of *Dubliners* disturbed its equilibrium and pessimism. The structure of *Dubliners* without 'The Dead' had been a deliberate, symmetrical 3-4-4-3 arrangement. The first three stories are of childhood: 'The Sisters', 'An Encounter' and 'Araby'. That is to say, the centre of consciousness in each story is that of a child. The subsequent four stories are of adolescence: 'Eveline', 'After the Race', 'Two Gallants' and 'The Boarding House'. This may go beyond the age of adolescence as now understood, but in Joyce's day the term seems to have carried the common specific meaning: 14 to 25 years old for a man, 12 to 21 years for a woman. The next four stories are of maturity: 'A Little Cloud', 'Counterparts', 'Clay' and 'A Painful Case'. Marriage and celibacy are at the centre of these stories. Finally, there are three stories of public life: 'Ivy Day in the Committee Room', 'A Mother' and 'Grace'. In each of these, the characters inhabit some public sphere of life: a committee room in Wicklow Street, a concert, a church. The bleak 'scrupulous meanness' of Joyce's plan and execution can be briefly illustrated. The first story of the fourteen begins with simony, the sin of buying and selling God's grace, and the last story of the fourteen ends with a priest describing Christ as a 'spiritual accountant'. The symmetry between all fourteen stories displays the repetition of connected themes: desire and money, adventure and friendship, religion and power, each of which paralyses another and paralyses the lives of the characters whose stories these are. In all fourteen stories the East is the index of new life, the West the index of death. The book in its version of 1906 ends on as downbeat a note of determined satire as Joyce could sound: the closing words of a sermon to a group of businessmen, 'I will set right my accounts.'

Nothing could be less like the uncertainties at the conclusion of 'The Dead' and, therefore, of *Dubliners* when the volume was published in 1914. The collection now displayed an unstable and asymmetrical arrangement: 3-4-4-3-1. The new instability of *Dubliners* is most strongly felt at the end, in the final paragraphs of 'The Dead', when the voice of the narrator and the voice of the character who has been under satiric judgement, Gabriel Conroy, become indistinguishable from each other in a blurred lyrical lullaby. At its conclusion, the text has erased a narrative point of view that might judge:

We are left pondering whether perhaps, in these final pages of 'The Dead', Joyce heard in the echoes of his 'moral history' a voice too much like his own sounding too much like the voice of judgement – too much, in fact, like Gabriel. Perhaps then he began to see and hear Dublin in a way that would stir him to write the more compassionate history he would come to call *Ulysses*.[112]

This destabilizing transformation, the insertion of 'The Dead' as the concluding story of *Dubliners*, was effected in 1907. And 1907 brings into focus transformations in the consciousness of Joyce. 'The Dead' is not the only piece of writing Joyce composed during that year. Indeed, on 16 September, four days before he finished writing 'The Dead', he would have been pleased to read in the local Trieste paper, *Il Piccolo della Sera*, his article 'Ireland at the Bar', the last of three substantial essays he submitted to the newspaper that year. Two other essays, 'Fenianism: the Last Fenian' and 'Home Rule Comes of Age', had been published in *Il Piccolo della Sera* on 22 March and 19 May, respectively. Joyce attached considerable importance to his newspaper articles and would later seek to have them published in book form. The title of the book was to be that of his September article, 'Ireland at the Bar'. These articles were, he insisted, about Ireland and the Irish people, written to instruct a European public misinformed by the British press. Also during this period, Joyce had addressed himself to the themes of Ireland, its history, culture and international image, in a lecture delivered in Trieste on 27 April 1907, 'Ireland: Island of Saints and Sages'. He had also prepared two other lectures: one (a version of a talk he had given as a student in Dublin) on the nineteenth-century nationalist poet James Clarence Mangan; the other (of which only a fragment survives) entitled 'The Irish Literary Renaissance'.[113]

These lectures and newspaper articles vividly show that Joyce was preoccupied during 1907 not simply with the delimited world of

Dublin that dominates so much of his major fiction, but with Ireland as a whole, with Ireland East and West, with its political and cultural history, with its revivalist agendas, and with its relationship to the world at large. It is these preoccupations that give scope, order, resonance and meaning to the text of 'The Dead'. 'The Dead' marks a moment of transformation in Joyce's consciousness of Ireland, a transformation in his politics, and in his aesthetics. In order to understand those transformations, in order to come to grips with why 'The Dead' is so unlike the other stories of *Dubliners*, we need to measure in some detail Joyce's extraordinary changes of mind during 1907.

Joyce's journalism divides into two main periods. The first is that of his reviewing for the *Daily Express* during his stay in Paris in 1902 and 1903. The second comprises the newspaper articles written in Trieste during and after 1907. In terms of Joyce's fiction, the two periods are divided by the writing of 'The Dead', with its wide canvas on Irish life, East and West, and its ironic, distancing portrait of a *Daily Express* reviewer, Gabriel Conroy. Joyce's reviews for the *Daily Express* had stated a definite politics. For example, his very first review in December 1902 is distinctly anti-nationalist, and as such is specifically contradicted by the politics of his Triestine journalism during and after 1907. The object of Joyce's antipathy in 1902 had been William Rooney, an activist in the Gaelic League and co-founder with Arthur Griffith of Cumann na nGaedheal and of the *United Irishman*. Rooney had died at the age of twenty-eight and Griffith did not delay in collecting, editing, introducing and publishing his young colleague's verse under the title *Poems and Ballads*. On the flyleaf of this book Rooney is designated as 'Fear na Muintire' (Man of the People), a phrase that had been one of his pseudonyms in the *United Irishman*. Griffith asserts in the introduction that 'Rooney was the greatest Irishman I have known or whom I expect to know. I do not claim him as the greatest of

Ireland's men of genius. Such a claim would be absurd. He was a man of genius, deep learning and ardent patriotism . . . he had established between his soul and the soul of Ireland a perfect communion.'[114]

With these words Griffith summarized the requirement of nationalism most troublesome to Joyce. The concept of a spirit or soul of the nation implies that cultural nativism would be the only effective means by which Ireland might survive British cultural dominance. It is precisely this essentialism which Joyce resisted. The flavour of Joyce's review of William Rooney can be caught in his judgement that the poems are 'a false and mean expression of a false and mean idea'. Even if Griffith thinks that these verses will 'enkindle the young men of Ireland to hope and activity, Mr Rooney has been persuaded to great evil'. It is no surprise that Griffith struck back in the face of such abuse. He published Joyce's review in the *United Irishman* as an advertisement for the book. His only emendation was the addition of a single word. Joyce had written (in an idiom to be taken up by Stephen Dedalus) that Rooney 'might have written well if he had not suffered from one of those big words which makes us so unhappy'. Griffith merely inserted the unspoken word: patriotism.[115]

It had been Lady Gregory who, at Joyce's request, had asked the *Daily Express* to send him books for review in 1902. Perhaps with the expectation that he would prove a sympathetic reader, the editor sent Joyce a copy of Lady Gregory's newest publication, *Poets and Dreamers: Studies and Translations from the Irish*, and asked him to review it. Joyce bit the hand that fed him. Under the title 'The Soul of Ireland' (quoting Griffith in revenge for Griffith quoting him) he provided the *Daily Express* with a corrosive review:

> This book, like so many books of our time, is in part picturesque and in part an indirect or direct utterance of the central belief of Ireland. Out of the material and spiritual

battle which has gone so hardly with her Ireland has emerged with many memories of beliefs, and with one belief – a belief in the incurable ignobility of the forces that have overcome her – and Lady Gregory, whose old men and women seem to be almost their own judges when they tell their wandering stories, might add to the passage from Whitman which forms her dedication, Whitman's ambiguous word for the vanquished – 'Battles are lost in the spirit in which they are won.'[116]

In *Ulysses* Buck Mulligan summarizes the review and its context to Stephen: 'O you inquisitional drunken jew jesuit! She gets you a job on the paper and then you slate her drivel to Jaysus.'[117] The *Daily Express* hesitated to print the review. Finally the editor allowed it to appear, but with one telling addition: Joyce's initials. Normal practice at the *Daily Express* was that all reviews were anonymous, but the editor contrived to distance himself from Joyce's opinions by identifying Joyce as the reviewer.

All this plays upon several ironies in both Joyce's 'The Dead' and Huston's *The Dead*. It is Gabriel Conroy's initials that betray him to Miss Ivors as a contributor to the *Daily Express*. More than that, the argument which Joyce had detected in Lady Gregory (about the nobility and innocence of the West of Ireland) animates Miss Ivors' politics of nativism. Joyce's review of Lady Gregory informs the text of 'The Dead', for Lady Gregory had cited as epigraph to her book Walt Whitman's 'A Song for Occupations':

> Will you seek afar off? you surely come back at
> last,
> In things best known to you finding the best, or
> as good as the best,
> In folks nearest to you finding the sweetest,
> strongest, lovingest,

> Happiness, knowledge, not in another place but
> this place, not for another hour but this hour.[118]

In answer to this plea on behalf of 'home', Joyce himself had cited in his review a different, more upbeat, poem by Whitman, the 'Song of Myself'. Indeed this poem, as cited by Joyce, contains the first hint of the title of 'The Dead', and the ironic analysis of failure that Joyce would give to his story in 1907:

> With music strong I come, with my cornets and
> my drums,
> I play not marches for accepted victors only, I play
> marches for conquer'd and slain persons.
>
> Have you heard that it was good to gain the day?
> I also say it is good to fall, battles are lost in the
> same spirit in which they are won.
>
> I beat and pound for the dead,
> I blow through my embouchures my loudest and
> gayest for them.
>
> Vivas to those who have fail'd!

In 'The Dead' it is Molly Ivors who repeats the Whitman/Gregory insistence that commitment to 'home' and to 'one's own' is more compelling than travel abroad. *Poets and Dreamers* survived Joyce's attempt to destroy it when Tony Huston's screenplay admitted it into the film in the form of one of its translations from the Gaelic, 'Donal Óg'.

Clive Hart, who acted as literary adviser to Huston on behalf of the Estate of James Joyce, has cautioned viewers of the film that 'Joyce would have hated the introduction into his story of a passage of Celtic revival literature'.[119] It is certain that Joyce, a reviewer at the *Daily Express* in 1902, would have hated such an insertion. It is quite uncertain, however, if Joyce, a columnist of *Il Piccolo della Sera*, author of 'The Dead' and of 'Ireland at the Bar' in 1907, would have objected to this piece of translation. In a strong sense Joyce's Triestine journalism is itself an act of translation between one culture and another, specifically an act of translation between the culture of Ireland and that of continental Europe. Early in 1907 the editor of *Il Piccolo della Sera*, Roberto Prezioso, to whom Joyce talked about Ireland and 'the ignorance that existed about Ireland on the continent',[120] requested articles that would discuss not only the British empire that ruled Ireland but also the Austrian empire that ruled Trieste. Joyce obliged.

There is some slight information available to us as to why Joyce in Trieste took a more compassionate view of Ireland. The author of the first fourteen stories of *Dubliners* faced a double embarrassment when the daughter of some of his Triestine friends mocked him to his face about Ireland. 'I felt humiliated', he wrote to his brother Stanislaus, 'at the little Galatti girl sneering at my impoverished country'.

> Sometimes thinking of Ireland it seems to me that I have been unnecessarily harsh. I have reproduced (in *Dubliners* at least) none of the attraction of the city for I have never felt at my ease in any city since I left it except in Paris. I have not reproduced its ingenuous insularity and its hospitality. The latter 'virtue' so far as I can see does not exist elsewhere in Europe. I have not been just to its beauty.

When confronted by his brother Charles with the assertion that *Dubliners* is not a book which betters its author's country or people, 'Jim replied that he was probably the only Irishman who wrote leading articles for the Italian press and that all his articles in "Il Piccolo" were about Ireland and the Irish people'.[121]

The representation of Ireland abroad is the central theme of Joyce's article, 'Ireland at the Bar', and a decisive motivation in his writing of 'The Dead'. Both depend upon memories about the West of Ireland told to Joyce by Nora. At the centre of 'The Dead' is Nora's account of Michael ('Sonny') Bodkin, who, like Michael Furey in Joyce's story, had died young. At the centre of 'Ireland at the Bar' is Nora's account of Myles Joyce, whose trial and execution stand as an analogy for Ireland's humiliation at the bar of international opinion. A multiple murder had been committed in 1882 on the border of Galway and Mayo. One of the defendants charged with that crime was a local man, Myles Joyce. Popular belief and much evidence indicated that he was innocent. However, Myles Joyce spoke only Gaelic. The trial was conducted in English. James Joyce, in 'Ireland at the Bar', gives a vivid rendering of the imagined scene in Green Street Courthouse, Dublin:

> The court had to resort to the services of an interpreter. The interrogation that took place through this man was at times comic and at times tragic. On the one hand there was the officious interpreter, on the other, the patriarch of the miserable tribe who, unused to civic customs, seemed quite bewildered by all the legal ceremonies.
>
> The magistrate said:
>
> 'Ask the accused if he saw the woman on the morning in question.'
>
> The question was repeated to him in Irish and the old man broke out into intricate explanations, gesticulating, appealing to the other accused, to heaven. Then, exhausted by the effort, he fell silent; the interpreter, turning to the magistrate, said:
>
> 'He says no, your worship.'
>
> 'Ask him if he was in the vicinity at the time.'
>
> The old man began speaking once again, protesting, shouting, almost beside himself with the distress of not

understanding or making himself understood, weeping with rage and terror. And the interpreter, once again replied drily:

'He says no, your worship.'

When the interrogation was over the poor old man was found guilty and sent before a higher court which sentenced him to be hanged. On the day the sentence was to be carried out, the square in front of [Galway] prison was packed with people who were kneeling and calling out prayers in Irish for the repose of the soul of Myles Joyce. Legend has it that even the hangman could not make himself understood by the victim and angrily kicked the unhappy man in the head to force him into the noose.

The figure of this bewildered old man, left over from a culture which is not ours, a deaf-mute before his judge, is a symbol of the Irish nation at the bar of public opinion. Like him, Ireland cannot appeal to the modern conscience of England or abroad. The English newspapers act as interpreters between Ireland and the English electorate which, though it lends an ear every so often, is finally irritated by the eternal complaints of the Nationalist deputies who, it believes, have come to their House with the aim of upsetting the order and extorting money. Abroad, Ireland is not spoken of except when some trouble breaks out there.[122]

The hanging of Myles Joyce in Galway prison and the death of Michael Furey share a common textual trace in 'The Dead'. Both recall and deconstruct a single canonical text: Lady Gregory's nationalist play *Cathleen Ni Houlihan* (1902), which W. B. Yeats had ascribed to himself and of which Joyce would have thought Yeats sole author. In the Yeats/Gregory play the Poor Old Woman, who symbolizes the 'Sovranty' of Ireland, sings a song of 'yellow-haired

Donough that was hanged in Galway'. When asked, 'What was it brought him to his death?' she replies, 'He died for love of me; many a man has died for love of me.' In Joyce's 'The Dead', Gretta, when questioned by Gabriel about the death of Michael Furey, offers the answer, 'I think he died for me.'

The identity and the difference between these two utterances are unmistakable. The irony of that identity and difference constitutes a forceful rewriting of Yeats and Gregory by Joyce. Gretta, unlike the Poor Old Woman of *Cathleen Ni Houlihan*, expresses some hesitancy: 'I think he died for me.' Also, Gretta has nothing to say about repetition, about the deaths of many men, 'some that died hundreds of years ago, and . . . some that will die tomorrow'.[123] There is for her no serial killing, just one incidental and dreadful loss. Gretta's exclamation is one of guilt, not of exultation. Joyce's account of Michael Furey in 'The Dead', taken together with his account of Myles Joyce in 'Ireland at the Bar', remembers the fate of 'yellow-haired Donough that was hanged in Galway'. Unlike Gregory and Yeats, however, Joyce refuses to identify a traumatic memory of the dead with an inevitable and ritual process of blood sacrifice. 'The Dead' is more ironic and less determinist than that. For Gabriel, in Joyce's story, is not merely a humiliated figure overwhelmed by the alleged native passions of the West. Joyce lends to Gabriel his own sentiments about Dublin's hospitality, his own love letters to Nora, his own book reviewing in the *Daily Express*, his own physical appearance.

'The Dead' is not a conversion narrative in which one set of convictions is replaced by another. It is a complex act of revision: revision of the authorial self, who had written and given a stable structure to the earlier bleak stories of *Dubliners*; revision of the values that separate Joyce's articles in the *Daily Express* from those in *Il Piccolo della Sera*; and revision of the demands of Irish revivalists, in the idiom of *Cathleen Ni Houlihan*, with their exultant cult of 'talking to the dead'. The narrative method of Joyce's 'The Dead' forbids the luxury of settled convictions. Viewers of Huston's film may enjoy some settled convictions that embarrass the story from which it derives. However, they are free to return to Joyce's story and, because of the contrast between story and film, be surprised at the power of the revisionary style of Joyce's text: a style that we may define as narrative irony without finality of judgement.

We may take as an exemplary instance Gabriel's recognition of Gretta on the stairs. In the film Gabriel's and the viewer's perception is immediate: 'the sixty-mile-an-hour pathos' of the cinematograph ensures that to see Gretta is to recognize her. In the story this act of recognition is an intricate sequence of self-correction. In shadow, the colours (terracotta and salmon pink) of Gretta's skirt appear monochrome and her upper body is lost in darkness. Even after Gabriel recognizes that it is Gretta, he cannot distinguish the exact quality of the music that can be faintly heard from above. Gabriel must decode the play of darkness, distance, misapprehension and reflection. Only after a process of revision can he know what he sees (and of course he still remains in the dark). So too, the reader. For example, in the final three paragraphs of the story, the reader must read and reread the sentences on the page, adjusting and readjusting the sense, according to the indeterminacy of whatever answer is provisionally given to the question: 'Who speaks these words?'

The film stabilizes these textual events and sometimes erases the gradual processes of perception and revision that characterize Joyce's story. That is the difference between the story and the film. The camera shows immediately the surfaces of things. The film, therefore, has served to rescue the story from readings that are overly symbolic or thematic: readings that have, for example, trivialized the life of the party or abstracted a cultural politics from the story's ending. The story survives the film, and reveals itself anew to those who turn back from the screen to read again Joyce's text. In the wake of viewing

Huston's film, readers are all the more likely to rediscover in 'The Dead' a textual, allusive, intricate narrative: a story that submits its narrator, its protagonist and its readers to deliberate and uncertain processes of misapprehension and self-revision.

CREDITS

Title: The Dead
Alternate Titles: Dubliners
Director: John Huston
Release Year: 1987
Production Company: Liffey Films
Vestron Pictures
Zenith Productions
Channel Four
Delta Film
Country: USA
Great Britain
German Federal Republic

Cast:

Anjelica Huston	Gretta Conroy
Donal McCann	Gabriel Conroy
Helena Carroll	Aunt Kate Morkan
Cathleen Delany	Aunt Julia Morkan
Ingrid Craigie	Mary Jane
Rachael Dowling	Lily
Daniel O'Herlihy	Mr. Browne
Donal Donnelly	Freddy Malins
Marie Kean	Mrs. Malins
Frank Patterson	Bartell D'Arcy
Maria McDermottroe	Molly Ivors
Sean McClory	Mr. Grace
Katherine O'Toole	Miss Furlong
Maria Hayden	Miss O'Callaghan
Bairbre Dowling	Miss Higgins
Lyda Anderson	Miss Daly
Colm Meaney	Mr. Bergin
Cormac O'Herlihy	Mr. Kerrigan
Paul Grant	Mr. Duffy
Redmond M. Gleeson	Night Porter
Brendan Dillon	Cab Man
Paul Carroll	2nd Young Gentleman
Dara Clarke	Young Lady
Patrick Gallagher	3rd Young Gentleman

Credits:

John Huston	Director
William J. Quigley	Executive Producer
Wieland Schulz-Keil	Producer
Chris Sievernich	Producer
Anne M. Shaw	Production Co-ordinator
Tom Shaw	Production Manager
Keith M. Sheridan	Post-production Supervisor
Lilyan Siervernich	Director of documentary crew
Tom Shaw	Assistant Director
John "Joe" Brooks	Assistant Director
Seamus Byrne	2nd unit assistant director
Gay Brabazon	2nd unit assistant director
Susan Carbery	2nd unit assistant director
Nuala Moiselle	Casting
Peggy Weber	Extras casting
Tony Huston	Script
James Joyce	Original short story
Fred Murphy	Photography
Randy Nolen	Camera Operator
Michael Coulter	Landscapes camera operator (Eire)
Lisa Rinzler	Documentary crew camera operator
Maurice Foley	2nd unit sp effects supervisor (Eire)
Candy Flanagin	Special Effects
Roberto Silvi	Editor
Stephen Grimes	Production Designer
J. Dennis Washington	Collaborating production designer
Arden Gantly	2nd unit art director (Eire)
Josie MacAvin	Set Decorator
Dorothy Jeakins	Costume designer
Jennifer L. Parsons	Costume supervisor
Jennifer Butler	Women's costumer
Marilyn Mathews	Women's costumer
Robert Pecina	Men's costumer
John McDonald	Men's costumer
Maeve Patterson	2nd unit wardrobe mistress (Eire)
Fern Buchner	Make-up
Keis Maes	Makeup design
Howard A. Anderson Company	Titles and opticals
Alex North	Music

Ann Stockton	Musician (solo harp)
Richard Bronskill	Orchestrations
Ken Wannberg	Music Editor
Len Engel	Music Recording
Dan Wallin	Music Recording
Paul Gleason	Choreography
Bill Randall	Sound Recording
Don Sanders	Documentary crew sound recording
Walt Martin	Documentary crew sound recording
Margaret Duke	Documentary crew sound recording
Robert Glass	Dialogue re-recording
Ken S. Polk	Music re-recording
John B. Asman	Effects re-recording
Marvin I. Kosberg	Supervising Sound Editor
James E. Nownes	Sound Editor
Anthony M. Palk	Foley (Editor)
Clive Hart	Literary adviser (James Joyce estate)

Running time:	83 minutes
Field length:	7642 ft or 2330 mtrs.
Colour code:	Colour
Colour system:	Foto-Kem

Notes

1   Christian Metz, 'Photography and Fetish', *October*, No. 34 (Fall 1985).

2   Richard Ellmann, *James Joyce* (Oxford: Oxford University Press, rev. ed. 1982), pp. 243–253; Jakob Lothe, *Narrative in Fiction and Film: an Introduction* (Oxford: Oxford University Press, 2000), p. 129; Denis Donoghue, 'Huston's Joyce', *New York Review of Books* (3 March 1988), p. 18; Clive Hart, *Joyce, Huston, and the Making of the Dead* (Gerrards Cross: Colin Smythe, 1988), p. 18; Vincent Cheng, *Joyce, Race, and Empire* (Cambridge: Cambridge University Press, 1995), pp. 128–147; Ruth Bauerle, 'Date Rape, Mate Rape: a Liturgical Interpretation of "The Dead"', in *New Alliances in Joyce Studies*, ed. Bonnie Kime Scott (Newark: University of Delaware Press, 1988), pp. 113–125.

3   Hugh Kenner, *Joyce's Voices* (London: Faber & Faber, 1978), pp. 15–16. Kenneth Burke also respects the story's 'loose ends': see '"Stages" in "The Dead"', in *Dubliners: Text, Criticism and Notes*, eds. Robert Scholes and A. Walton Litz (Harmondsworth: Penguin Books, 1976), p. 414.

4   Hart, p. 18.

5   James Joyce, Vol. 2, *Letters*, eds. Stuart Gilbert and Richard Ellmann (New York: Viking, 1966), pp. 166–167.

6   Tony Huston, a presentation on the filming of *The Dead* given at a public forum at the Curtis Institute of Music on 14 June 1989, in conjunction with a national conference, 'James Joyce in Philadelphia' (hereafter, Tony Huston, Presentation, 1989). I am grateful to Professor Timothy Martin, Rutgers University, for an audiotape of the presentation.

7   John Francis Lane, 'A Magical Adieu', *Irish Times* (9 September 1987), p. 12.

8   Michael Gray, *Stills, Reels and Rushes: Ireland and the Irish in Twentieth-Century Cinema* (Dublin: Blackhall, 1999), pp. 174–177; Tom Milne, 'The Dead', *Monthly Film Bulletin*, Vol. 54, No. 647 (December 1987), pp. 355–356.

9   Charles Hunter, '*The Dead* Opens the Festival', *Irish Times* (29 October 1987), p. 12.

10 John Hill, 'The Future of European Cinema: the Economics and Culture of Pan-European Strategies', in *Border Crossing: Film in Ireland, Britain and Europe*, eds. John Hill, Martin McLoone and Paul

Hainsworth (Belfast: Institute of Irish Studies, 1994), pp. 53–80. John Huston had himself urged the Irish government to found an Irish Film Board: see Lawrence Grobel, *The Hustons* (New York: Avon Books, 1989), p. 591.

11   Martin McLoone, *Irish Film: the Emergence of a Contemporary Cinema* (London: British Film Institute, 2000), pp. 33–84. For recurrent genre representation of Ireland on screen, see also *Contemporary Irish Cinema: from* The Quiet Man *to* Dancing at Lughnasa, ed. James MacKillop (New York: Syracuse University Press, 1999); Lance Pettitt, *Screening Ireland: Film and Television Representation* (Manchester: Manchester University Press, 2000); and for similar genre representation on the international and national stage, see Nicholas Grene, *The Politics of Irish Drama* (Cambridge: Cambridge University Press, 1999).

12   Wieland Schulz-Keil, 'Appreciating Huston: the Life in the Works', in *Perspectives on John Huston*, ed. Stephen Cooper (New York: G. K. Hall, 1994), pp. 205–215.

13   Lane, p. 12; and see also Yung, 'The Dead', *Variety* (2 September 1987), p. 14.

14   *The Letters of John Keats*, ed. Maurice Buxton Forman (Oxford: Oxford University Press, 1947), p. 305.

15   Grobel, *passim*; for Irish citizenship, see John Huston, *An Open Book* (New York: Knopf, 1980), p. 234.

16   David Desser, 'John Huston: a Biographical Sketch', in *Reflections in a Male Eye: John Huston and the American Experience*, eds. Gaylyn Studlar and David Desser (Washington: Smithsonian Institute Press, 1993), pp. 201–206.

17   Huston, *An Open Book*, pp. 239–241; Tony Huston, Presentation, 1989.

18   Grobel, p. 2; John Huston highlights the dedication to Maricela Hernandez in the documentary, Lilyan Sievernich (dir.), *John Huston and the Dubliners: On the Set of 'The Dead'* (Germany: Liffey Films, 1987).

19   Manny Farber, *Negative Space: Manny Farber on the Movies* (New York: Praeger, 1971), p. 33.

20   David John Wiener, '*The Dead* : a Study of Light and Shadow', *American Cinematographer* (November 1987), pp. 62–68. The essay includes detailed technical analysis of lighting the film by Fred Murphy. See also Moylan Mills, 'Huston and Joyce: Bringing "The Dead" to the Screen', in MacKillop, p. 120–127: Mills credits

Stephen Grimes and Dorothy Jeakins for 'a muted palette of beiges, tans, and dark grays with cream and rose highlights, a combination perfectly in tune with the faded wallpaper in the Morkan apartment. This design creates a sense of looking at an ancient sepia photograph and provides an exact correlation with the nostalgic, reflective mood of the story' (p. 126).

21 Lesley Brill, *John Huston's Filmmaking* (Cambridge: Cambridge University Press, 1997), pp. 223–224.

22 David Bordwell and Kristin Thompson, *Film Art: an Introduction* (New York: McGraw-Hill, 1993), pp. 82–84, 261–269; William Luhr, 'Tracking *The Maltese Falcon*: Classical Hollywood Narration and Sam Spade', in *Close Viewings: an Anthology of New Film Criticism*, ed. Peter Lehman (Tallahassee: Florida State University Press, 1990), pp. 7–22.

23 Tony Huston, Presentation, 1989.

24 Hart, pp. 11–12.

25 Donoghue, p. 19.

26 For the argument that Joyce's story has of itself a filmic structure, see Paul Deane, 'Motion Picture Techniques in James Joyce's "The Dead"', *James Joyce Quarterly*, Vol. 6 (1968/69), pp. 231–236.

27 Joyce, *Letters*, Vol. 2, pp. 146, 165, 217.

28 Grobel, pp. 13, 17.

29 Tony Huston, Presentation, 1989.

30 Ellmann, *James Joyce*, pp. 252–253.

31 The discovery of old Irish story patterns in Joyce's story begins with John V. Kelleher, 'Irish History and Mythology in James Joyce's "The Dead"', *The Review of Politics* (1964), pp. 414–433; Joyce's access to popular versions of old Irish materials is demonstrated in Maria Tymoczko, *The Irish Ulysses* (Los Angeles: University of California Press, 1994); Paul Muldoon elaborates on these in *To Ireland, I* (Oxford: Oxford University Press, 2000).

32 Ellmann, *James Joyce*, p. 231.

33 Ellmann, *James Joyce*, pp. 245–246.

34 Gerard Gould, *New Statesman* (27 June 1914), pp. 374–375, reprinted in *James Joyce: the Critical Heritage*, Vol. 1, ed. Robert H. Deming (London: Routledge & Kegan Paul, 1970), pp. 62–63.

35 Ellmann, *James Joyce*, p. 301.

36 See Christian Metz, 'Photography and Fetish', *October*, No. 34 (Fall 1985), pp. 76–93, and Roland Barthes, *Camera Lucida: Reflections on Photography*, trans. Richard Howard (London: Jonathan Cape, 1982).

For an account of this debate, see Martin Jay, *Downcast Eyes: the Denigration of Vision in Twentieth-Century French Thought* (Los Angeles: University of California Press, 1993), pp. 484–491.

37 Gideon Bachmann, 'How I Make Films: an Interview with John Huston', *Film Quarterly*, Vol. 19, No. 1 (Fall 1965), pp. 3–13, reprinted in Cooper, p. 112.

38 Cooper, p. 107.

39 Ronan Farren, 'McCann Lands Lead in Huston Movie', *Sunday Independent* (30 November 1986), p. 5.

40 Charles Hunter, 'Huston Brings "The Dead" to Life' [An interview with Maria McDermottroe], *Irish Times* (26 February 1987), p. 12.

41 Wiener, p. 63.

42 Grobel, p. 9.

43 Tony Huston, Presentation, 1989.

44 Press Package, Chris Sievernich Filmproduktion, 1987.

45 John Orr and Colin Nicholson, eds., *Cinema and Fiction: New Modes of Adapting, 1950–1990* (Edinburgh: Edinburgh University Press, 1992), p. 3.

46 Tim Pulleine, 'A Memory of Galway: *The Dead*', *Sight and Sound*, Vol. 57, No. 1 (1987/88), pp. 67–68.

47 Donoghue, p. 18.

48 Bachmann, pp. 100, 102.

49 James Agee, 'Undirectable Director', *Life* (18 September 1950), pp. 23–28, reprinted in Studlar and Desser, p. 263.

50 James Naremore, 'Return of the Dead', in Cooper, pp. 198–199.

51 All transcriptions from the film are from Roberto Rossellini (dir.), *Voyage to Italy* (Italy: Sveva Film, 1953). For the advantages to Irish cultural studies of exploring *Voyage to Italy*, and other such texts that view Ireland indirectly and from the outside, see Nicholas Miller's forthcoming monograph, *Lethal Histories: Modernism, Ireland and the Memory of History* (Cambridge University Press).

52 Stanislaus Joyce, 'The Background to *Dubliners*', *The Listener*, Vol. 51 (25 March 1954), pp. 526–527.

53 Quoted in Peter Brunette, *Roberto Rossellini* (Los Angeles: University of California Press, 1987), p. 159. For a fine analysis of *Voyage to Italy*, see Peter Bondanella, *The Films of Roberto Rossellini* (Cambridge: Cambridge University Press, 1993), pp. 98–111.

54 Brunette, p. 156.

55 Ezra Pound, '*Dubliners* and Mr James Joyce', *Egoist*, Vol. 1, No. 14 (15 July 1914), p. 267.

56   Brill, *John Huston's Filmmaking*, p. 208.
57   Mills, pp. 122–124.
58   Quoted in Bachmann, p. 102.
59   Tony Huston, '*The Dead*: A Screenplay' (unpublished) (Los Angeles: Liffey Films, 1986), pp. 44–45 (hereafter Tony Huston, Screenplay).
60   Tony Huston, Presentation, 1989, mentions 'the shadow of 1916'. For a study of the generation represented in 'The Dead' (albeit at a level below that of the élite), see Senia Paseta, *Before the Revolution: Nationalism, Social Change and Ireland's Catholic Élite, 1879–1922* (Cork: Cork University Press, 1999).
61   Michael Levenson, 'Living History in "The Dead"', in *The Dead*, ed. Daniel R. Schwartz (New York & Boston: Bedford Books, 1994), pp. 163–177.
62   Joyce himself, at a later date, ironically calls into question the Englishness of Shakespeare's work when he jokingly remarks that almost all Shakespeare's 'characters come from abroad or afar': James Joyce, *Occasional, Critical, and Political Writing*, ed. Kevin Barry (Oxford: Oxford University Press, 2000), p. 164.
63   Levenson, p. 177.
64   Frank O'Connor, 'Work in Progress', in *Dubliners: Text, Criticism and Notes*, eds. Robert Scholes and A. Walton Litz (Harmondsworth: Penguin Books, 1976), p. 312.
65   These judgements can be found in Scholes and Litz, pp. 408, 410, 412.
66   Kevin Rockett, Luke Gibbons and John Hill, *Cinema and Ireland* (New York: Syracuse University Press, updated with postscript, 1988), pp. 262–263.
67   Contrast Cheng, *Joyce, Race, and Empire*, pp. 136–137, with Cheng, 'Authenticity and Identity: Catching the Irish Spirit', in *Semicolonial Joyce*, eds. Derek Attridge and Marjorie Howes (Cambridge: Cambridge University Press, 2000), pp. 240–261.
68   Schwartz, p. 77.
69   Unsigned review of *The Dead*, *Screen International*, No. 619 (26 September 1987), p. 27.
70   Donoghue, p. 18.
71   Quoted in Brill, *John Huston's Filmmaking*, p. 208.
72   Brill, *John Huston's Filmmaking*, p. 195.
73   Brill, *John Huston's Filmmaking*, p. 216.
74   Allen Tate, '"The Dead"', in Scholes and Litz, p. 408.
75   Tony Huston, Screenplay, pp. 28–30.

76   Cheng, *Joyce, Race, and Empire*, p. 143; Levenson, p. 176, claims 'That Gretta loved Michael Furey before he [Gabriel] met her, that she has felt a passion keener than any he has known . . .'

77   Margot Norris, 'Not the Girl She Was at All: Women in "The Dead"', in Schwartz, pp. 190–205.

78   James Joyce, *Poems* and *Exiles*, ed. J. C. C. Mays (Harmondsworth: Penguin, 1992), pp. 346–347.

79   Unsigned review of *Dubliners*, *Times Literary Supplement* (18 June 1914), p. 298.

80   Tony Huston, Screenplay, pp. 84–87.

81   Some critics have noticed the absence of 'lust' in the film and its presence towards the end of the story in Gabriel's mind on his way from party to hotel. There has, however, been consensus that the story ends without sex. See, for example, Hart, pp. 17–18, and Bauerle, pp. 124–125.

82   These judgements can be found in Scholes and Litz, pp. 409, 415–416, 422, 443.

83   Cheng, *Joyce, Race, and Empire*, p. 147.

84   Ellmann, *James Joyce*, p. 252.

85   John Paul Riquelme, 'For Whom the Snow Taps: Style and Repetition in "The Dead"', in Schwartz, pp. 219–233.

86   Tony Huston, Presentation, 1989.

87   Naremore, p. 205. Critics who explore the subversive uncertainties of this narrative voice include Vincent P. Pecora, '"The Dead" and the Generosity of the Word', *PMLA*, Vol. 101, No. 2 (1986), pp. 233–245 and Robert Spoo, 'Uncanny Returns in "The Dead"', in *Joyce: the Return of the Repressed*, ed. Susan S. Friedman (Ithaca: Cornell University Press, 1993), pp. 89–113.

88   Elizabeth Butler Cullingford, 'Phoenician Genealogies and Oriental Geographies: Joyce, Language, and Race', in Attridge and Howes, pp. 219–239.

89   Kenner, pp. 15–16, christens this narrative device 'The Uncle Charles Principle', after a character in *A Portrait of the Artist as a Young Man*. See also Lothe, p. 136.

90   Seymour Chatman, *Story and Discourse: Narrative Structure in Fiction and Film* (Ithaca: Cornell University Press, 1978), p. 105. For the comparability of montage in the narrative structure of novel and cinema, see Sergei Eisenstein, 'Dickens, Griffith, and the Film Today', in *Film Theory and Criticism*, eds. Gerald Mast and Marshall Cohen (Oxford: Oxford University Press, 1985), pp. 370–380.

91 Orr and Nicholson, p. 2.
92 Frank Pilipp, 'Narrative Devices and Aesthetic Perception in Joyce's and Huston's "The Dead"', *Literature/Film Quarterly*, Vol. 21, No. 1 (1993), pp. 61–68.
93 Lothe, pp. 154-155.
94 Hart, p. 18.
95 Brill, *John Huston's Filmmaking*, p. 226.
96 John Simon, 'Death and Soul-Death', *National Review* (22 January 1988), pp. 64–66.
97 Rockett, Gibbons and Hill, p. 263.
98 Brian Pendreigh, *On Location: the Film Fan's Guide to Britain and Ireland* (Edinburgh & London: Mainstream, 1996), pp. 224–226.
99 Marjorie Howes, '"Goodbye Ireland I'm going to Gort": Geography, Scale, and Narrating the Nation', in Attridge and Howes, pp. 58–77.
100 Tony Huston, Screenplay, p. 18.
101 Tony Huston, Presentation, 1989.
102 Andrew Sarris, 'John Huston', in *The American Cinema: Directors and Directions, 1927–1968* (New York: Dutton, 1968), p. 158.
103 Pauline Kael, 'Circles and Squares', in Mast and Cohen, p. 550.
104 Lesley Brill, '*The Misfits* and the Idea of John Huston's Films', in Cooper, p. 153.
105 Gaylin Studlar, 'Shadowboxing: *Fat City* and the Malaise of Masculinity', in Studlar and Desser, p. 184.
106 Martin Rubin, 'Heroic, Antiheroic, Aheroic: John Huston and the Problematic Protagonist', in Studlar and Desser, pp. 142–143, 148ff.
107 Rubin, p. 154. For Huston's reception in French cinema, see Robert Benayoun, *John Huston: La Grande Ombre de l'Aventure* (Paris: Lherminier, 1985).
108 Unsigned review of *Dubliners*, *Times Literary Supplement* (18 June 1914), p. 298.
109 Sarris, p. 158.
110 Grobel, p. 478.
111 Florence L. Walzl, 'Gabriel and Michael: Conclusion of "The Dead"', in Scholes and Litz, pp. 423–424.
112 Bruce Avery, 'Distant Music: Sound and the Dialogics of Satire in "The Dead"', *James Joyce Quarterly*, Vol. 28, No. 2 (1991), pp. 473–483.
113 Joyce, *Occasional, Critical, and Political Writing*, pp. 108–147.
114 William Rooney, *Poems and Ballads* (Dublin: United Irishman, 1902), p. x.

115   'An Irish Poet', *Daily Express* (11 December 1902), quoted in Joyce, *Occasional, Critical, and Political Writing*, pp. 74–76. Griffith's advertisement promptly appeared in *United Irishman* (20 December 1902).

116   Joyce, *Occasional, Critical, and Political Writing*, pp. 75–76.

117   James Joyce, *Ulysses*, ed. Hans Walter Gabler (Harmondworth: Penguin Books, 1986), 9.1158–1160.

118   See Walt Whitman, *Leaves of Grass* (1855), and Lady Gregory, *Poets and Dreamers: Studies and Translations from the Irish* (Dublin: Hodges Figgis, 1903).

119   Hart, p. 13.

120   John McCourt, 'Joyce on National Deliverance: the View from 1907 Trieste', *Prospero: Rivista di Culture Anglo-Germaniche*, Vol. 5 (1998), pp. 27–46. For the fullest account of this period in Joyce's life, see John McCourt, *The Years of Bloom: James Joyce in Trieste, 1904–1920* (Dublin: Lilliput, 2000).

121   Joyce, *Letters*, Vol. 2, pp. 166–167, 316.

122   Joyce, *Occasional, Critical, and Political Writing*, pp. 145–146.

123   See Ellmann, *James Joyce*, pp. 248–249; W. B. Yeats, *Collected Plays* (London: Macmillan, 1966), pp. 82–83. For Gregory's *Cathleen Ni Houlihan* and her attachment to men in gaol, see Lucy McDiarmid, 'The Demotic Lady Gregory', in *High and Low Moderns*, eds. Maria DiBattista and Lucy McDiarmid (Oxford: Oxford University Press, 1996), pp. 212–218. There is, indeed, an uncanny likeness between a passage in Lady Gregory's 1900 essay 'The Felons of Our Land' and the closing phrases of 'The Dead': 'In Ireland the peasant has always before his eyes, on his own cottage walls or in his white-washed chapel, the cross, the spear, the crown of thorns, that tell of what once seemed earthly failure, that tells us He to whom he kneels was led a felon's death.' See Lady Gregory, *Selected Writings*, eds. Lucy McDiarmid and Maureen Waters (Harmondsworth: Penguin, 1995), p. 278. See also Grene, pp. 65–66.

Bibliography

Agee, James. 'Undirectable Director'. *Life* (18 September 1950): 23–28.

Anonymous. 'Dubliners'. *Times Literary Supplement* (18 June 1914): 298.

Anonymous. '*The Dead*'. *Screen International*, No. 619 (26 September 1987): 27.

Attridge, Derek, and Marjorie Howes. *Semicolonial Joyce*. Cambridge: Cambridge University Press, 2000.

Avery, Bruce. 'Distant Music: Sound and the Dialogics of Satire in "The Dead"'. *James Joyce Quarterly*, Vol. 28, No. 2 (1991): 473–483.

Bachmann, Gideon. 'How I Make Films: an Interview with John Huston'. *Film Quarterly*, Vol. 19, No. 1 (1965): 3–13.

Barthes, Roland *Camera Lucida: Reflections on Photography*, trans. Richard Howard. London: Jonathan Cape, 1982.

Bauerle, Ruth. 'Date Rape, Mate Rape: a Liturgical Interpretation of "The Dead"', in Scott, 1988. 113–125.

Benayoun, Robert. *John Huston: La Grande Ombre de l'Aventure*. Paris: Lherminier, 1985.

Bondanella, Peter. *The Films of Roberto Rossellini*. Cambridge: Cambridge University Press, 1993.

Bordwell, David, and Kristin Thompson. *Film Art: an Introduction*. New York: McGraw-Hill, 1993.

Brill, Lesley.'*The Misfits* and the Idea of John Huston's Films', in Cooper, 1994. 145–160.

——. *John Huston's Filmmaking*. Cambridge: Cambridge University Press, 1997.

Brunette, Peter. *Roberto Rossellini*. Los Angeles: University of California Press, 1987.

Burke, Kenneth. '"Stages" in "The Dead"', in Scholes and Litz, 1976. 410–416.

Chatman, Seymour. *Story and Discourse: Narrative Structure in Fiction and Film*. Ithaca: Cornell University Press, 1978.

Cheng, Vincent. 'Authenticity and Identity: Catching the Irish Spirit', in Attridge and Howes, 2000. 240–261.

——. *Joyce, Race, and Empire*. Cambridge: Cambridge University Press, 1995.

Cooper, Stephen. Ed. *Perspectives on John Huston*. New York: G. K. Hall, 1994.

Cullingford, Elizabeth Butler. 'Phoenician Genealogies and Oriental Geographies: Joyce, Language, and Race', in Attridge and Howes, 2000. 219–239.

Deane, Paul. 'Motion Picture Techniques in James Joyce's "The Dead"'. *James Joyce Quarterly*, Vol. 6 (1968/69): 231–236.

Deming, Robert H. Ed. *James Joyce: the Critical Heritage*. 2 vols. London: Routledge & Kegan Paul, 1970.

Desser, David. 'John Huston: a Biographical Sketch', in Studlar and Desser, 1993. 201–206.

DiBattista, Maria, and Lucy McDiarmid. Eds. *High and Low Moderns*. Oxford: Oxford University Press, 1996.

Donoghue, Denis. 'Huston's Joyce'. *New York Review of Books* (3 March 1988): 18–19.

Eisenstein, Sergei. 'Dickens, Griffith, and the Film Today', in Mast and Cohen, 1985. 370–380.

Ellmann, Richard. *James Joyce*. Oxford: Oxford University Press, rev. ed. 1982.

Farber, Manny. *Negative Space: Manny Farber on the Movies*. New York: Praeger, 1971.

Farren, Ronan. 'McCann Lands Lead in Huston Movie'. *Sunday Independent* (30 November 1986): 5.

Friedman, Susan F. Ed. *Joyce: the Return of the Repressed*. Ithaca: Cornell University Press, 1993.

Gould, Gerard. '[Review of *Dubliners*]'. *New Statesman* (27 June 1914): 374–375.

Gray, Michael. *Stills, Reels and Rushes: Ireland and the Irish in Twentieth-Century Cinema*. Dublin: Blackhall, 1999.

Gregory, Lady Augusta. *Poets and Dreamers: Studies and Translations from the Irish*. Dublin: Hodges Figgis, 1903.

——. *Selected Writings*. Eds. Lucy McDiarmid and Maureen Waters. Harmondsworth: Penguin, 1995.

——. 'West Irish Folk Ballads'. *The Monthly Review* (October 1902): 134–5.

Grene, Nicholas. *The Politics of Irish Drama*. Cambridge: Cambridge University Press, 1999.

Grobel, Lawrence. *The Hustons*. New York: Avon Books, 1989.

Hart, Clive. *Joyce, Huston, and the Making of the Dead*. Gerrards Cross: Colin Smythe, 1988.

Hill, John. 'The Future of European Cinema: the Economics and Culture of Pan-European Strategies', in Hill, McLoone and Hainsworth, 1994. 53–80.

Hill, John, Martin McLoone and Paul Hainsworth. Eds. *Border Crossing: Film in Ireland, Britain and Europe*. Belfast: Institute of Irish Studies, 1994.

Howes, Marjorie. '"Goodbye Ireland I'm going to Gort": Geography, Scale, and Narrating the Nation', in Attridge and Howes, 2000. 58–77.

Hunter, Charles. 'Huston Brings "The Dead" to Life [An interview with Maria McDermottroe]'. *Irish Times* (26 February 1987): 12.

——. '*The Dead* Opens the Festival'. *Irish Times* (29 October 1987): 12.

Huston, John. *An Open Book*. New York: Knopf, 1980.

Huston, Tony. Presentation on the filming of *The Dead* given at a public forum at the Curtis Institute of Music on 14 June 1989, in conjunction with a national conference, 'James Joyce in Philadelphia'.

——. '*The Dead*: A Screenplay'. Los Angeles: Liffey Films, 1986. [Unpublished].

Jay, Martin. *Downcast Eyes: the Denigration of Vision in Twentieth-Century French Thought*. Los Angeles: University of California Press, 1993.

Joyce, James. *Dubliners*. Ed. Jeri Johnson. Oxford: Oxford University Press, 2000.

——. *Letters*. Eds. Stuart Gilbert and Richard Ellmann. 3 vols. New York: Viking, 1966.

——. *Occasional, Critical, and Political Writing*. Ed. Kevin Barry. Oxford: Oxford University Press, 2000.

——. *Poems* and *Exiles*. Ed. J. C. C. Mays. Harmondsworth: Penguin Books, 1992.

——. *Ulysses*. Ed. Hans Walter Gabler. Harmondsworth: Penguin Books, 1986.

Joyce, Stanislaus. 'The Background to *Dubliners*'. *The Listener*, Vol. 51 (25 March 1954): 526–527.

Kael, Pauline. 'Circles and Squares', in Mast and Cohen, 1985. 541–552.

Keats, John. *The Letters*. Ed. Maurice Buxton Forman. Oxford: Oxford University Press, 1947.

Kelleher, John V. 'Irish History and Mythology in James Joyce's "The Dead"'. *The Review of Politics* (1964): 414–433.

Kenner, Hugh. *Joyce's Voices*. London: Faber & Faber, 1978.

Lane, John Francis. 'A Magical Adieu'. *Irish Times* (9 September 1987): 12.

Lehman, Peter. Ed. *Close Viewings: an Anthology of New Film Criticism*. Tallahassee: Florida State University Press, 1990.

Levenson, Michael. 'Living History in "The Dead"', in Schwartz, 1994. 163–177.

Loomis, C. C. Jr. 'Structure and Sympathy in Joyce's "The Dead"', in Scholes and Litz 1976. 417–422.

Lothe, Jakob. *Narrative in Fiction and Film: an Introduction*. Oxford: Oxford University Press, 2000.

Luhr, William. 'Tracking *The Maltese Falcon*: Classical Hollywood Narration and Sam Spade', in Lehman, 1990. 7–22.

McCourt, John. 'Joyce on National Deliverance: the View from 1907 Trieste'. *Prospero: Rivista di Culture Anglo-Germaniche*, Vol. 5 (1998). 27–46.

——. *The Years of Bloom: James Joyce in Trieste 1904–1920*. Dublin: Lilliput, 2000.

McDiarmid, Lucy. 'The Demotic Lady Gregory', in DiBattista and McDiarmid, 1996. 212–228.

MacKillop, James. Ed. *Contemporary Irish Cinema: from* The Quiet Man *to* Dancing at Lughnasa. New York: Syracuse University Press, 1999.

McLoone, Martin. *Irish Film: the Emergence of a Contemporary Cinema*. London: British Film Institute, 2000.

Mast, Gerald, and Marshall Cohen. Eds. *Film Theory and Criticism*. Oxford: Oxford University Press, 1985.

Metz, Christian. 'Photography and Fetish'. *October*, No. 34 (Fall 1985): 76–93.

Miller, Nicholas. *Lethal Histories: Modernism, Ireland and the Memory of History*. Cambridge: Cambridge University Press, 2001.

Mills, Moylan. 'Huston and Joyce: Bringing "The Dead" to the Screen', in MacKillop, 1999. 120-127.

Milne, Tom. 'The Dead'. *Monthly Film Bulletin*, Vol. 54, No. 647 (1987): 355–356.

Muldoon, Paul. *To Ireland, I*. Oxford: Oxford University Press, 2000.

Naremore, James. 'Return of the Dead', in Cooper, 1994. 197–206.

Norris, Margot.'Not the Girl She Was at All: Women in "The Dead"', in Schwartz, 1994. 190–205.

O'Connor, Frank. 'Work in Progress', in Scholes and Litz, 1976. 304–315.

Orr, John, and Colin Nicholson. Eds. *Cinema and Fiction: New Modes of Adapting, 1950–1990*. Edinburgh: Edinburgh University Press, 1992.

Paseta, Senia. *Before the Revolution: Nationalism, Social Change and Ireland's Catholic Élite, 1879–1922*. Cork: Cork University Press, 1999.

Pecora, Vincent P. '"The Dead" and the Generosity of the Word'. *PMLA*, Vol. 101, No. 2 (1986): 233–245.

Pendreigh, Brian. *On Location: the Film Fan's Guide to Britain and Ireland*. Edinburgh & London: Mainstream, 1996.

Pettitt, Lance. *Screening Ireland: Film and Television Representation*. Manchester: Manchester University Press, 2000.

Pilipp, Frank. 'Narrative Devices and Aesthetic Perception in Joyce's and Huston's "The Dead"'. *Literature/Film Quarterly*, Vol. 21, No. 1 (1993): 61–68.